Being A Man According To The Bible

Written and illustrated by Jeff Todd

Contents

Introduction

There is a code that most folks from the male species live by that is given to us from birth. It's not written down anywhere for us to read, study and practice. It's more like a chemical – it's part of our chromosomes and DNA – that flows through our bodies, our blood and brains. It tells us how we should act in all situations, how we should think and how to express ourselves in our environments. It's like a survival mechanism created just for men. It helps us to mingle in with other men and become productive – working together – to make this world a better place. However, for the women, this code can create relationships that they would rather not be part of.

Women don't understand this 'man code', but try to live with it every day with their husbands, co-workers and in their social life. It's a complex system that will cause a woman to either ignore it, accept it or simply choose to stay away. Many have tried to learn more about this code, but usually get frustrated and just move on.

Being a man in this world means living by the man code. We are judged by our fellow men that we socialize with daily. They will give you strange looks when you attempt to do something that is considered 'not manly'. You can be shunned from the manly community and lose your imaginary 'man card' for doing anything that only females are known to do. Following the man code is a serious thing.

Since there is not a written document in place, we have to ask, "Where did this 'man code' come from? Where did it originate? And what exactly is in there?"

And because if there is no written document, who's to say that it didn't get changed along the way? Maybe this man code that men have been living by for hundreds of years is wrong. What then?

It could be why women don't understand us. Maybe that's why marriages don't work out and relationships don't last. We need to go to a more reliable source for information.

Today, we take a closer look at this 'man code' and compare it to what the Bible says. The Bible has been around for hundreds of years and is one of the ways God, our Creator, communicates with us. Maybe we can discover what He intends for us, as men, to really be. I mean, He created man and had the original plan for manhood - that would make Him the only source we should really look to and we can find the details in the Bible.

My prayer today is that we can learn something about ourselves – the good, the bad and the ugly – and apply what we receive from God's Word to our lives. I hope that we make the appropriate steps to become better people – better men. I believe that God has a perfect plan for us and wants us to live productive lives. He wants us to have great relationships with our wives, kids, families and friends.

If we take a stand today to look away from the world for advice and look to Him, our life will be better. He can make those changes in our lives if we allow Him. It's really up to us.

Thanks for reading this today. I hope you receive something from it and are blessed.

A Reflection Of A Man

The Day I Left Home

I believe in every male teenager's mind, they are looking forward to the day when they can officially be called a man.

I mean, they survived through nine years of being in a single-digit age category. Then, they get promoted to a double digit number, and half way through it, they are called teenagers. After enduring those stressful short years, they get promoted to manhood. It's the big day they have been waiting for – armed with peach fuzz whiskers and raging hormones.

For me, being a man happened on July 25, 1987. This was my 18th birthday.

I didn't achieve this status by accomplishing anything major. I didn't spend my childhood years training to hunt wild game in treacherous woods with a pocket knife. I didn't kill a bear with my bare hands. I didn't have to bungee jump off the side of a mountaintop. I think the hardest thing I had to do was keep my room clean and do my daily chores, which I really didn't do too well anyway. All I had to do was turn 18. That's it! Or at least I thought.

A year prior to my birthday, I remember my parents constantly nagging me to get a job and to start looking for a new place to live because they had big plans for my bedroom. I think they wanted to turn it into a storage room and fill it with all of their treasures they had accumulated from years worth of bargain shopping. To speed the moving process, they quickly turned from being loving parents to evil landlords by charging me rent every week. This was something new to me and very disturbing. And to make matters worse, I was given additional duties like cleaning my bathroom and washing my own clothes. Things were getting out of hand. I mean, I had just finished twelve years of school and now it was my time to relax. But, these new changes taking place in my life was messing up my plans, so I had to do something quick.

Fortunately for me, I had a friend who was living at home with his mother. She was a single Mom that took care of her two sons. She was wonderful. She would manage their home, wash their clothes, cook nutritious meals every day while working a full time job. And the great thing was that she didn't charge them for this service. She would get stressed at times, but overall she seemed more than happy to do it.

Her oldest son was in his mid-twenties and had a great job. He was doing pretty good financially because he always had money, a nice truck and could do whatever he pleased. He had freedom. This was the life that I wanted., too.

I didn't have to pay rent for too long. My friend, after hearing me complaining all the time, asked me if I wanted to come move in with them. They had a spare bedroom with a private bathroom available, so I quickly jumped on this once-in-a-lifetime opportunity. I would have been foolish not to. I packed my bags and moved immediately. I don't think I gave a notice to my current landlords. I was gone.

Before I go any further with this story, let me set the record straight. I wasn't expecting a free ride. I was now a man and knew that I had to do my share by carrying my load. If someone was going to wash my clothes, do all of the cleaning and cook my meals, the least I could do was offer a financial token of my appreciation. I gave my friend's Mom the same deal that I was paying before I moved. And as an added bonus, I would even cut the grass. No problem. I was being financially smart because I was getting more for my rent money.

Life was grand for a while. I was finally living the dream of being out on my own. I could do as I pleased. However, I never abused this freedom and showed my appreciation by doing everything I could as a team player. Being a man was everything I expected it to be and more. I was happy.

As months passed, I learned quickly that in order to get on top of my financial ladder, I had to get a better job. Paying rent while working at a fast food restaurant didn't work together too well. I couldn't stop paying rent because I would be going against my manly duty. The only option I had was to find a job that paid more. I had responsibilities now and if I wanted to improve myself, I would need more money. It was a no-brainer and I quickly began my job search.

My First Real Job

I have always worked. As a young child, I would do small jobs like cutting a neighbor's grass in exchange for monetary gain. And on the days I wasn't doing manual labor, I would scrounge the neighborhood in search of soda bottles that I would take to the local convenience store for pocket change. I always had money and knew how to earn it. Money was a goal that kept me from being lazy. Actually, it helped me develop entrepreneurial traits at an early age.

I remember going to school with a large heavy book bag that I would carry around with me at all times. It wasn't full of books. The book bag was more of a safe and convenient way to carry my inventory of candy that I would sell to my customers on a daily basis. Yes, my customer database consisted of teachers, bus drivers and fellow students. And they all had one thing in common - they had money and wanted my products. I offered a good assortment.

I think they looked forward to seeing me every day. They knew that they could buy bubble gum, candy bars and breath mints from me at the same price they could get them from the store. I learned the strategy of buying wholesale and in bulk to drive my prices down. They loved it and were happy to pay me for my value-packed service. It was a win-win for the both of us.

There's a big difference in earning money as a child as compared to making money as a man. Child money doesn't pay for rent. It won't pay for much of anything in the real world. To make it in this world, you have to have a real job. It's one of those places you have to go to every day, do everything they tell you to do without complaining and wait a week to receive a financial reward for all of your efforts. Of course, you use this reward to give to everyone that you are obligated to – such as landlords, bills, food and entertainment – all of the things we got for free as a child, but now are paying dearly for. And then you repeat the same process the following week. It's a never-ending struggle.

Being a man at 18 meant that I would have to find a job that paid on a regular basis. Not one of those 'get paid every two weeks for working only 2 to 3 days a week' kind of jobs. It would have to be a job where I could earn enough money to pay for my current necessities while being able to save for the next level of life. I was a smart man and thought a lot about my future.

Fortunately for me, I only had to apply to a few jobs before I landed one. This was back in the good old days when you could actually visit a company and apply right there on the spot. We didn't have to go through a Temp Service or apply online because the 'www' stuff didn't exist yet. We didn't have to waste countless hours of online data entry on a job application that people won't read anyway. Getting a job back in my day was more of a personal effort that required talking to real people and filling out real paperwork with a real pen.

I just so happened to show up at the right company at the right time with the right skills. At this job, I later learned that the true reason I was hired was because I had arms and legs. It's funny to think about now, but the lady in charge of hiring me was short one person in her department. She was frustrated and told the Human Resource Department, who was holding my application, that she didn't care who they hired as long as they had arms and legs. Fortunately, for me, I had both and got the job.

Of course, I learned that in order to keep the job, I had to make some personal changes. The first one was getting in the habit of waking up early in the morning. It was hard to do at first because teenagers like to stay up late at night and sleep til noon, but I finally got into the habit. Alarm clocks are great investments when you're in the working world. The second change I had to make, which hurt me the most, was that I had to change my youthful choices of clothing that I wanted to wear. I could no longer dress the way I wanted to. I had to fit in with the new working environment.

Fashion Choices
Sometimes You Have To Conform

All my life I refused to be like every one else. If the latest trend was silky shirts and jogging pants, I would purposely wear a t-shirt and blue jeans. I went against the system. I wore a fishing hat simply because people either didn't wear one or they wore fashionable ball caps with popular logos on them. Not me. I wanted to be my own person, not a human product of the latest fashion trend.

1980'S FASHION

WELL,.... ALMOST.

I will admit, this gets you noticed. Most of the time it's in a negative way. Back in the 1980's, when acid wash jeans made the scene, I wore regular jeans with holes in the knees. I was laughed at and told many times by my teachers to start wearing nicer clothes or I would be sent home. Dressing like this was unacceptable. Oddly enough, when the 1990's rolled around, jeans with holes became fashionable. You could buy them with holes already on them. Some marketing guy came up with the name 'distressed' and the idea took off. And so did I. I had to change my style again.

In the working world as a young man, you learn quickly that you have to go with the system. Money has now became the driving

18

force and you have to 'fit in' in order to keep a happy balance in life. If you go against the system, you can actually cut into your income. I had to change the way I thought about things. To be a man at that time meant making adjustments in order to maintain peace and live a productive life.

In this new job that I received, I had to dress to code. I had to wear whatever was acceptable in the new working environment. I had to put aside my personal thoughts and ideas in order to conform with the environment that was now paying me my paycheck. It wasn't easy.

Young In Love
Lessons In Manhood

She was the most prettiest thing I had ever seen. We were sitting in the wooden pews of an old country church that was about ten minutes from my home. She looked back at me with her beautiful big eyes. I couldn't resist her stares. At that moment, I wanted to spend the rest of my life with her. And a few years later, we climbed aboard the Love Train and hit the tracks going full speed. Thirty years later, I'm proud to say that we are still on that train. And every time we look back, we remember that it wasn't always a smooth ride.

The early years were only successful because we made sacrifices for each other. This meant making adjustments in how we did things. If something I did made her mad, I would change it because I loved her. She would do the same for me. Some things took many attempts because you can't expect a person to change over night.

I have always been an independent person. I have been trained through the School of Hard Knocks to take care of myself. My belief had always been that I am responsible for me and no one else. Just because I got married doesn't mean that I now have to take care of another person. Marriage, to me at that time, was more like a partnership where 'you take care of you' and 'I will take care of me'. We'll live together, love one another and do all of the fun things

MARRIED... YET, INDEPENDENTLY MAINTAINED.

that married couples do, but each of us is responsible for our own maintenance and upkeep. It seemed like the perfect plan to me.

I had a job. She had a job. We could take care of ourselves — independently. There were some duties that were known for being a man's job or a woman's job. We were taught early in life that some things men and women did not do. Men don't cook. Women don't cut grass. We were fine with that. She was taught that women don't take the trash out. Instead, they let it overfill until the man gets frustrated and takes it out. Going against the beliefs of some of my friends, I was taught that men can clean house, but not to the extreme of major dusting and deep cleaning. This could wait a month or two. By this time, the woman would get frustrated and do it herself.

We had to do a lot of fine tuning in our relationship. Many things were solved by constantly nagging and arguing with each other. And that was fine. In our relationship, arguing was acceptable because not only did it solve problems, it would also lead into something fun in the bedroom. We both were willing to make sacrifices and go against our own ways of thinking. If we weren't arguing, it would mean that we were doing things right. We were living on love and willing to change to keep our love growing. We didn't want to waste any of our 'love' time together arguing with each other.

One of the early lessons in our marriage was learning that we were created to help each other. I can remember my young wife being sick with a stomach virus. She was pitiful. One morning she decided to puke right in the middle of the floor. She couldn't wait, walk a few steps and take it to the bathroom. Oh no! She let that junk come right on out and land in the middle of the floor. I even waited for her to clean it up, but learned that she was too sick and weak to do it.

"Eww! That was nasty. Are you going to get that up?"

"I don't feel good. I don't think I can."

"Hmm... you sure? It's kind of gross. Do you want me to get you a broom and a mop?"

To get that stink out of the room, I ended up cleaning it up by myself. It wasn't my puke, but I knew it had to be done. A part of my pride was broken that day. I also gained sympathy and learned how much I truly loved her because no man in their right mind would do this for their wife.

Another early lesson that comes to mind was on a touchy topic, "What's Mine Is Yours and What's Yours Is Mine". This lesson blew me away to the point that I had to call my mother for advice. I didn't know how to handle it.

"Mom, you are not going to believe this."

"What's wrong, honey? You can tell me."

"She wants me to use my money, that I worked hard for, to buy her those 'monthly' woman things that you wear. I don't think it's fair."

"But, honey..."

"You don't understand. This is my money. My money! Why should I have to spend it on THAT?"

Needless to say, I bought them. It was either buy them or let her bleed to death. And I loved having her around.

It's easy to laugh at a story like this now. I look back and realize how selfish I was. I know now that marriage is about sacrificing and basically putting your spouse and their needs above your own. As a man, I know I should do everything possible to take care of my wife and she does the same for me. It was a learning process that came with years of mental struggles and anguish.

Early Role Models
Setting The Bar For Manhood

A young boy growing up learns from his surroundings. When it comes to becoming a man, he learns from the male figures that he sees on a regular basis. This can be from his home, his neighborhood or from television. These men influence their lives – whether it's positive or negative. They make an impact on the child's life which helps them in the development process. It can be good or bad.

There weren't many male role models in my home. My mother was a single parent doing the best she could to raise me. I think she did a great job considering what she had to work with. The lack of a father-figure could have been a bad thing for me, but it wasn't. I was just very fortunate to have a great mother. According to statistics, a percentage of kids without a father in the home:

- Grow up poor
- Abuse drugs and alcohol
- Have behavioral problems
- Make bad grades in school
- Become criminals at a young age
- Become parents in their teenage years

I can't say that all of these things happened to me. Yes, I grew up poor, but at the time, I didn't know it. All of my friends in my neighborhood were poor, too. And honestly, I had everything I needed. I had a great childhood. If a kid is poor, it can force them to be creative when it comes to playing games and entertaining themselves. If not, they will get bored. I always had something to do.

In school, I was always on the honor roll. I made good grades. Me and my choice of friends were at the top of our class. We were involved in school activities that only kids with good grades could take part in. I didn't have a problem with school. I enjoyed the challenge. Having friends that were smart gave me the incentive to be smart, too. Maybe their influences from other men passed down to me through them. If that makes sense.

I lived in a poor section of town. It was called a village, not because we lived in huts with roofs made from palm tree leaves. I think it was because the houses were small and real close together. The rent was cheaper and so was the construction of the homes. They were barely insulated.

I can remember the cold winters. Cold air would find its way through the walls and the cracks of the windows. Being poor, you couldn't fix the problem properly – you had to improvise with what you had. The only way we could solve the problem was by folding newspapers and sticking them in the cracks. These houses were so hard to heat. I remember many times having to get dressed for school under my bed covers. We had gas heaters that had a hard time heating the house when it was very cold outside. If you stood closer to the heater, you could get warmer, but you risked a chance of catching on fire. Literally!

The houses were all walking distance to an old cotton mill that was built in the late 1800's. I imagine back in those days, these mills would make an extra income from their employees by building them these cheap homes that were conveniently a walking distance away and then charge them rent for this convenience. And now a hundred years later, these houses are still standing and still as shoddy as they were back then.

It wasn't all bad living there. We had luxuries that the rich kids didn't have. We had a creek, railroad track, ballpark and a convenience store. It was Paradise Island for a poor kid. Plus, it was better than being homeless.

Having a creek was hours of entertainment for the neighborhood kids. At that time, kids really didn't need adult supervision. We could be trusted and were allowed to enjoy ourselves and be social with other kids. We had freedom to explore our world and learn from our own mistakes. I can remember a science lesson I learned as a kid from studying water currents and the amount of force they have as they push your fragile

drowning body downstream. I also learned that I couldn't swim. And as an added bonus, I learned what happens when this water current pushes you into a bee's nest that was built on the side of the creek bank. Thankfully, I didn't drown but I did have bee stings to remind me to never do this again.

Train tracks are great for transporting goods across long distances. They were also great for walking on and learning about nature. A poor child explorer could walk for miles and find wonderful treasures such as the skeletal remains of animals. It was another science project that we all could experience. We learned how to examine a dead animal body to determine the species by its head shape, number of teeth and size. We also found rare artifacts left behind from the local drunks that decided to take a therapeutic walk on the railroad track such as beer bottles and even clothing. You never knew what you would find.

The local ball park was a good place for sporting events. It was also a cool place for the poor neighborhood kids to play. I imagine if I wanted to start a baseball league, I would buy some land in the poorest section of town because the land would be cheaper. I could make more money from the city parents that would sign their kids up because my overhead costs would be lower. I would also build a fence around it to keep the poor kids away that lived nearby. I wouldn't want to lose any future paying customers by letting the riff-raff in.

Fortunately, for us poor kids, we knew how to climb a fence. We had enough kids in the neighborhood to form two teams and we could play ball against each other. To make the game more interesting, someone would sneak into the building behind home plate and turn on the scoreboard. Or if we needed more balls, we would borrow them. They had a ton of them inside the locked equipment building. It was just like the big leagues. Of course, when a real game was scheduled, we couldn't play. We would wait behind the fence until they left and would start back up again. We would look around first to see if any baseball supplies were left behind. You can never have enough bats and balls – especially free ones.

The neighborhood I grew up in had many single-parent households where the mothers were usually the ones raising their children. It also had a few of the older folks – some were retired and living off their social security checks. And then there were a few normal families that had both a father and a mother. The place where I lived had variety.

Les – A Strange Man, But Interesting

One of my early neighborhood influences was my step-grandfather, Les. He was retired and lived down the street. Even though he and my grandmother were divorced, I still considered him as my grandfather. He was a very unique person and lived by himself. I stayed with him during the Summer months so that my mother could work.

His story was a weird one. Back in the day, my grandmother was looking for a mate and decided to find one in the Classifieds Section of a popular magazine. I guess she struck gold when she stumbled across an ad from a gentleman living in Wisconsin. She lived in Georgia, but through letters and phone calls, they finally hook up and decide to settle down in my neighborhood. Of course, this was before I was born.

I've been told that their relationship was unstable. If they ever got into a big argument, she would divorce him. Later, as they reconciled their differences, she would marry him again. I have been told that this process happened six times. I know from on-hand experience, that he was a stern man and set in his ways. He was always right no matter how wrong he could have been. He had a code that he lived by and no one could change it – not even my grandmother.

As a kid, every morning was always the same routine. My Mom would drop me off and I would sit in the kitchen while he was waking up. He would do his regular bathroom duties, get dressed and head to the kitchen. He would always fry up a runny egg with a side order of toast. We would dip the toast into the runny egg junk and eat it. We did this every morning. It was the only breakfast food available. No cereal. No grits or oatmeal. Just runny eggs and toast. That was it and was part of his daily schedule.

He also smoked a pipe and used Prince Albert Tobacco from a can. After breakfast, he would fire that thing up and the smoke would fill the kitchen. Kids these days would consider this a health hazard from breathing in secondhand smoke. But, for me, it was kinda cool and gave him the look of sophistication. He was a like a short hairy Sherlock Holmes that knew how to do anything. When he puffed on his pipe, chances were, he was thinking about something intellectually cool. Of course, he would lose his thoughts when he coughed. This would cause the hot ashes to fly out and burn holes in his T-shirt.

He always had something for me and him to do around his house. We were either working on various projects he had or we were sitting down and playing card games. We would also work together on his hobbies of stamp and coin collecting. There was always something to do. He got free labor and I learned a lot from him.

He had a garden. It was small, but it seemed so huge. I guess because it had so much stuff growing in it. The house he lived in sat on a small patch of land, but he used most of it for growing things. He had a plum tree. He grew peanuts, strawberries and just about anything you would find at the grocery store. He also grew muscadines – these are grapes that grow commonly in the South. He knew a lot about farming and was willing to teach me.

Everything he grew in his garden was larger than normal. He wouldn't buy fertilizer from your local feed and seed store. He would import manure himself by raking it and bagging it up from somebody's barn and transporting it to his house from the trunk of his 1970 Ford Galaxie 500. It was all 100% natural. I guess that would make the fruits and vegetables he grew organic and healthy. I never understood why his strawberries tasted so good considering they were deeply saturated in animal crap. But, I kept eating them anyway.

He was a self-maintained man. He never needed for anything. And if he did, he would figure out a way to make it himself or build it with his own hands. This was way before YouTube was invented. I guess he was never afraid to try something new and believed in himself and his abilities to experiment. I always thought that was a great trait to have.

Les was also a cook. He would cook home-cooked meals – not like a bachelor, but like a man with real cooking skills. I imagine, for a man with unstable relationships, he would have to learn to cook in order to survive. I learned through him that cooking wasn't just a woman's job. A man could do it, too. He could bake his own bread, make desserts from scratch and made some of the best homemade beef jerky I had ever tasted. He would also use the muscadines that he grew for making homegrown wine. I remember sneaking samples of it and it was good. His house always smelled like food – like a good home-cooked meal. It gave a pleasant feeling when you walked through the doors.

He did his own home maintenance and auto repairs, too. He wouldn't call a professional if he needed something worked on. He would do it himself. He had tools. Even though he was retirement age, he wouldn't let his age or disabilities hold him back. He would climb his roof, crawl under his car and cut his own grass with a small push mower. Sometimes he would let me do it for him and pay me for it. I think he did this for my benefit.

The strange thing to me that I remember was that he kept notebooks. One was for keeping track of his mileage and gas consumption in his car and the other was for monitoring the kilowatt hours from the electric meter box on the side of his house. I'm not really sure of his purpose for doing it, but he did it on a regular basis. Maybe he was was trying to save money on energy costs because he was very frugal with his money. Or maybe, if he felt that the power company was trying to overcharge him, he would whip out his notebook and set them straight. He watched every penny.

Les was a Christian man. He loved God and watched church services on television. I would watch them with him sometimes. I don't recall him going to a church building on Sunday. I don't think he really liked people too much. He tried his best to live the life that Jesus taught from the Bible. One thing was for sure was that he didn't like thieves, especially the ones that stole from him.

He had a plum tree in his front yard that would produce some of the largest plums that I had ever seen. They were almost the size of a baseball. Because I asked for permission, he would let me pick as many as I wanted. Of course, you could only eat two because plums have a way of putting you on the toilet with a bad case of diarrhea. Eating a bunch of plums while riding long distances on your bicycle would not be a good idea. But, the plums were there and available to me any time I wanted one. They were also readily available to the neighbors that would sneak into his yard and take them without asking. He would catch them sometimes and run them off. Finally, he had enough. He was tired of people stealing them and decided to do something about it. One day, he cut the tree down. No more plums.

RIP

PRINTED ON
KODAK PAPER

It had more to do with the standard that he chose to live by. If a man works hard to produce something good for himself and his community, why should he allow others to steal it from him? He chose to take it out of the equation and cut it down. It was a sad day for the entire neighborhood.

Les was a good man and would do anything for anybody. He served our country in World War 2 and I guess life had made him very tough-skinned. He always looked angry, but once you started talking to him, you realized he was a very nice guy. I will miss him.

Buddy – The Local Businessman

Our small town had a local convenience store. Everything was generally higher priced than what you would pay for it in the city. However, some of the people living in the town couldn't afford cars or the gas to go to one to shop for the better deals. They would walk to the convenience store instead.

My mother bought our groceries there - mostly because we didn't own a car. We were frequent customers and the store owner knew us on a personal basis. His name was Buddy and would deliver our groceries to our home. He was a good person.

Buddy was a real Southern gentleman that wore overalls on a daily basis. It was his business attire and everyday work-wear. The interesting thing to me about him was that he could buy something and resell it at a higher price. I was fascinated by this. Sometimes he would share with me some of his business tips on making a profit. I saw this firsthand when I would bring him the empty soda bottles I had found around the neighborhood. He would pay me 7 cents each and told me that when he accumulated enough of them, he would take them to the local bottling company downtown and sell them for 10 cents a piece. That's a whopping 3-cent profit! It may not sound like much, but when you have a room in your store dedicated to recycled bottles, freely brought to you from money-hungry kids, this amount could grow rapidly. I simply enjoyed the idea of bringing in something I found for free and making money from it. It was a great business concept for a poor kid.

Another cool thing about Buddy was that he seemed to know a lot about the value of precious metals. Sounds odd, I know. But, as a kid in search of wealth and the golden ticket to financial freedom, I could always take anything metal that I found from my neighborhood journey to him to determine if the item was a precious metal. He had this magic chemical in a small bottle that, when he applied it to the metal's surface, it would change colors if the item was gold or silver. If it did, he would offer to buy it from me. He would then sell it to someone else for a profit.

Buddy was a humble business man that I looked up to. His store still stands today in my old neighborhood. There's an old faded painted Pepsi sign on the side of the building that still bears his company's name. Even though the store is boarded up and empty, I can still recollect all of the good memories I had there.

The Evans' Brothers

There was a family that lived next door to us that always considered me as part of their own. I would spend a lot of time there playing with their kids, eating their groceries and learning family values from their way of living. Their home consisted of a father and mother with four kids, plus... a grandmother, an uncle and an aging chihuahua that would bite your ankles every time you entered their door. I hated that stupid dog.

This family was the perfect example of how a family should be because they all worked together. Every one had a job to do. The men worked their regular jobs at the power company, yet they would come home and take care of their manly duties, too. The two men were brothers and shared the workload by working together on everything - cutting grass, working the garden and repairing their vehicles right there in their driveway. I remember the time they decided to build a brick shop building with a bonus bedroom in the attic. They built it in their backyard and it only took them a few weeks to get it done. Teamwork made it possible.

They used it to do manly things like building rabbit houses for the many rabbits they had. They would breed them for the sole purpose of eating them for dinner. I didn't know this bit of important information until after I ate one thinking it was barbecued chicken. It tasted good.

They would also use the building for making their own lead sinker weights by melting scrap metal and pouring it into molds for using when they went fishing. As a child, I would watch them make them. I thought it was cool. The fumes would stink and bring tears to your eyes, but it didn't matter. This was way before lead poisoning and the harmful effects of being exposed to it became popular on the news. I'm sure it was safer back then.

Sometimes the men would cook together in their yard from an open fire and steel pot. It was an exclusive technique that only hillbillies did, but these guys were masters in fine cuisine and knew a lot about different ways of cooking. I remember one special evening that changed my life forever. They were cooking something one day and asked if I would like to try a little sample. Even though it smelled like raw sewage, I gave it a shot anyway and took a sip from their tarnished spoon. The texture was strange and chewy, but it was definitely something I had never had before. Needless to say, this was the first and last time that I had ever tried eating chitterlings. I didn't know what it was until they told me – after I ate it. I do not understand how someone can eat a chicken's intestines knowing what flows through them. But hey! Whatever!

The Evans' brothers were real men. They were hunters and fishermen that proudly prepared their 'catch' in the privacy of their own yard. If there were buckets lying around their yard, chances were, there would be guts and fish heads in them. They taught me at a young age how to properly gut a catfish with a knife, pair of pliers and a wooden board with a nail in it. This is what separated the men from the boys.

Every evening you could always count on the brothers doing something constructive in their yard. You would also find them doing it with a beer can in their hands. They enjoyed drinking beer. I guess it was a great way to unwind from a hard working day. It would begin as soon as they came home and would stop when they went to bed. On special occasions, you would see one of the brothers roaming around the neighborhood mumbling to himself. When this happens, you would know that he either drank too fast or he had drank too much. We were told to just leave him alone. He would be OK by the next day.

The Evans' Brother taught me a lot about being a man. They taught me about the importance of working together to accomplish goals. Oddly enough, I also learned that it's OK to try new things, regardless of how it looks or smells. The brothers will be missed.

Family Influence – Uncles Make An Impact
My mother had four sisters and a brother. Sometimes we would go and visit them. You can learn a lot by simply being around family. Boys can pick up a few traits by watching how their uncles acted around them.

My Uncle William was a hard worker. He would get up early for work and come home to work again around the house. He liked building things. He was very crafty. If my aunt wanted something made, she would simply tell him what she wanted and he would buy some wood and make it. No big deal. This was before websites, such as Pinterest, were ever invented. I don't think he ever re-purposed old pallets. He built cool stuff, such as their house, the fences that surrounded it and a cool playhouse for my cousins.

He always wanted to make my aunt happy. I'm sure in today's world, he would have been considered 'whipped', but he did those things because he loved her. And when he finally found some free time for himself, he would work on his hobby cars. He had an old truck, 1957 Chevy and a 1970's Corvette Stingray. They were parked along the driveway and always looked like a work in progress. I don't think he ever got to finish them.

He was always busy, but he was happy. Every thing he did, he did for his family. He wasn't self-centered because his world seemed to be revolved around them. He died a happy man with love in his heart.

My Uncle Ed was a business man with a manufacturing facility in Atlanta. His company produced wire display racks that you would see in most stores that would hold magazines and newspapers. The thing that I remember most about him was how analytical he was. He thought about things first before following through with an action. He also seemed to know a lot about everything. I guess it was because he would take the time to learn all of the details.

When I got my driver's license at 16, he was there to teach me how to drive a truck with a 5 speed manual transmission (aka stick shift). But, before just allowing me to hop in his truck and start driving, he gave me a detailed lesson on how it all works; how the transmission works, what happens when you shift the gears and why pressing the clutch is so important. I later learned that pressing the clutch is an art, and if it's not done correctly, you could snap the necks of everyone riding in the car with you. I got yelled at a lot by him for not learning to do this correctly sooner. I always liked to look at my feet when I did it and would forget to look at the road. But, Uncle Ed believed that learning to do something involved learning everything about it – the how's and the why's.

I worked for him at his Atlanta company for a few months. One of my jobs was to drive the company truck to make various deliveries. It would have been a great job if I were good with driving directions. This was a sad time before navigational systems, internet and cell phones with driving apps. If you wanted to drive somewhere, you had to look at a map. If you couldn't read a map properly, you would have to listen to your Uncle giving you all of these left and right turns in places that you have never been before. If you didn't listen or couldn't focus on what he was saying, you would get lost. If you didn't write it down, you would get lost. Needless to say, I would always get lost. I would have to find a pay phone on the side of the road and call him to get back on track. This involved getting fussed at for not listening. He couldn't understand how someone could get lost from following his simple driving directions. This is the only job that I've ever had that I quit. The pressure was too much.

This is the reason that I always drive today with my navigator on at all times – even on small local trips. Uncle Ed taught me the importance of learning the details about everything. It's not enough just knowing how to do something. You need to know everything about it. Even though he's gone, I still apply his wisdom to my everyday life.

Hollywood – It's Influence on Kids

My parents, when they were married, enjoyed going to the drive-in theater. To them, I'm sure it was more than just watching a movie. Back in the day, a drive-in theater was a cool place to park and make out while a movie was playing on a large screen in the distance. Every car had it's own personal speaker that you would attach to your driver's side window. If you were a young married couple without a babysitter, you could still go out on a date. You would take your child with you and make them play on the playground. Parents could entertain themselves within the comfort of their own car. Your child wouldn't mind because all of the other parents parked there were doing the same. The playground had many kids to play with.

I was one of those kids that played on the playground while the movie was showing. The movies I remember the most were the Bruce Lee movies. I enjoyed watching them and would mimic those Kung Foo moves I saw on the big screen. While the windshields of all the parked cars were fogged up, I would be outside with my new friends doing Karate with hand chops and flying drop kicks. This would later pay off when I had to prove to the neighborhood kids how tough I was. I would wear a bath robe with a belt that tied at the waist. The kids either thought I

was a Kung Foo Master or a kid with mental issues. Either way, they knew to keep their distance.

Another Hollywood icon was Steve Austin (aka The Six Million Dollar Man). He had bionic super strength that cost six million dollars to create. Of course, times have changed and now just about any surgery you get will cost about the same. But, back in the day, it was expensive and The Bionic Man was super cool. I liked him so much that I joined the Six Million Dollar Man Club and had the action figure with the hole in the back of his head for seeing far distances. I was a serious fan. Even today, I am still a member of the Six Million Dollar Man Club with an autographed certificate.

At that age, every time I ran, I would have the same super cool strength. Sometimes I would even make the noises that came from having bionic speed. If you were a child from the 1970's, you would know the sound I am talking about. It just made you feel like you were running fast, even if other kids were running faster than you.

When the 1980's rolled around, I had other Hollywood actors that may have had an influence. I had a thin mustache because it was cool and manly, just like Magnum P.I. Sometimes I would wear a bandanna around my head that may have been subconsciously done from watching Rambo a few times. Wearing big necklaces and saying 'I pity the fool' was definitely from watching too many episodes of The A-Team with Mr. T. All of these were manly-men from my childhood day. They symbolized toughness, strength and super coolness. Every boy wanted to have these traits, too.

Music was a big thing in the 1980's. Most kids, like me, had a portable radio that we would carry around with us at all times. It wasn't just a radio. It had big speakers and would 'BOOM'. That's why we called them a 'boom box' instead of a portable radio. It just sounded cooler. Plus, it looked very cool when you walked around with this heavy thing on your shoulders.

We would walk the neighborhoods with it and would play our favorite tunes at full volume. Cassette tapes were popular because, not only could you play a full album of any particular artist, you could create and record your own collection of music from various artists on one cassette tape – called a mix tape. Your mix tape had to contain the best music – a compilation of the best songs from the best artists from the genre that you liked best.

If you had a cool bus driver, they would allow you to bring your boom box on the bus to share your tunes with everyone riding with you to school. The negative side of this was that everyone played their radios, too – at the same time. This would cause bus wars because everyone tried to 'over volume' everyone else. The biggest boom box always won. It wasn't always a war over volume, it was a war over the genre of music being played.

A popular music on my bus was Rap. Today this genre is called Old School Hip Hop. It contained artists such as Ice-T, Slick Rick, Fat Boys and other groups I didn't really care about. I didn't listen to Rap. I called it CRAP. I listened to the cool stuff such as Van Halen, Whitesnake, Def Leppard, Ratt, AC/DC and U2. Some of these were considered Hair Bands from a genre called Hair Metal because the singers had, of course, big hair. They also wore makeup, lipstick and colorful spandex pants, which was considered very manly in my day. These were the ones I played proudly on the bus. This was part of my arsenal to drown out their 'annoying' sounds of Rap. It would cause arguments and fights. Eventually our bus driver put a stop to it – no more boom boxes.

As kids, we were influenced by our music choices. You could see it in how we acted and the clothes we chose to wear. Music was a major part of our lives. We even had a dedicated channel on cable TV that played nothing but music videos 24/7 – MTV (Music Television). It set the standards for our generation and for who we would be as human beings.

I know my wife was saturated in 80's fashion with her big hair, leg warmers and Member's Only jacket. Everywhere we went, she had to fluff her hair up and spray it down with a gallon of hair spray. I always called it her Wilma Flintstone Forehead Fluff. In order to kiss her, when we dated, I would have to lift her hair up off of her face. But, at least she was fashionable.

Music and music videos set the standards for how we acted and dressed back then. Even though most of the music artists looked like women according to today's standards, our generation knew the difference and were proud to dress and be just like them.

Learning To Be A Man
Simple Lessons In Life

Learning to be a man was more than just observing people. You had to go through life experiences, too. You would take what you have seen from other men and practice it for yourself in your own individual circumstance.

School was the perfect place to practice being manly as a child, especially among your fellow classmates and friends. Back in my day, there were certain things you did and didn't do. Here are a few examples:

The Manly Greeting – You Could Do (In School)

- You were allowed to shake hands, high-5 and punch each other on the arm. Handshakes were to be firm (not wimpy or soft). High-5's were forceful to the point that a loud sound was heard. Arm punches were powerful. If you left a bruise on their arm, you were manly. If you broke their humerus bone, you were the king of all things manly.

The Manly Greeting – You Could Not Do (In School)

- Guys did not hug one another, especially in public. Hugs were acts of affection and real men were not to be affectionate at all.
- You couldn't use your hands or feet to touch any guy anywhere below the belt. An exception would be in fighting where your opponent was stronger than you. You would basically kick them in their private parts so that they would bow over. This would be immediately followed by an upper cut to their face.

THE GOLDEN RULE:
ALWAYS LEAVE A SPACE BETWEEN TWO URINAL USERS!

Restroom Etiquette For Young Men (In School)

- The most important rule was to never use a urinal that was directly beside another male. If this meant holding your bladder until he finished, that's what you had to do.
- No talking while using a bathroom stall. Period. Conversation could begin only when both parties were finished and at the hand washing area.
- If two males enter a bathroom at the same time, it was a race to finish quickly. Staying too long together could totally mess up your reputation in school.
- No grunts or 'ahh' sounds while in the bathroom. This would mean you were doing something else other than what most people do in a bathroom. People doing this would be ridiculed for the rest of their life.

Competitive Sports For Young Men (In School)

- Unlike today, fighting in the 80's was not necessarily a violent act upon one another. It was more of a competitive sport where one male would compete against another. It had three stages: the argument, the battle and the winner (being the last man standing). Fights were generally held at school or around convenient public places such as parking lots of local stores. These places would generate a crowd and that was their purpose. These spectators would share the victories and losses with your fellow classmates. No one ran away from a fight – unless they wanted to be labeled a 'chicken' with eternal embarrassment.

- Since video games were just coming out and very expensive to buy, kids would play 'hand' games to compete with one another. These games included Mercy, The Thump Game, Bloody Knuckles and Thumb War for the guys. In many cases, both winners and losers would receive swollen or bloody knuckles. It was just part of the game and considered very manly.

Dating (In School)

Real men didn't chase after girls. Girls would chase after them. But, to be girl-worthy, guys had to always be cool. The best way to do this was to act like at least one of the latest popular celebrities from Hollywood.

If the girls liked the movie Grease, you had to look and act like John Travolta (Danny) from the movie. Slicking your hair back, wearing leather and smoking cigarettes would make you an instant hottie among the ladies. If you couldn't afford all of the accessories, you could simply wear a Grease t-shirt, wiggle your hips and hope they got the idea. If a girl was a fan of the movie The Breakfast Club, you could be either a jock or a rebel, but not the geek. The geek wasn't the cool one, even though many of us fell into this category anyway.

The girls would initiate the dating process by writing a simple letter to you that asked, "Do you like me? Yes? Or no?" The letter would be neatly folded with a pull-out tab for easy opening. As an option, she may spray it with a popular perfume to get your attention. It would definitely be covered with hand-drawn hearts and big bubbly lettering.

If you replied back with a 'yes', the two of you would be considered a dating couple. Hopefully, you were a good writer because this would be the major way of communicating with her. Every letter she sends you must be replied to or she will think you were mad or cheating on her. The telephone was the communicating device of choice at night time. It was sorta like today's cell phone, but it had a chord that attached to a wall. This gave you limited walking ability depending on the length of the chord. She would mostly do the calling, unless she called and left you a message to call her back. It would be important for you to call her back immediately or she would think you were mad or cheating on her. Phone calls could last for several hours — regardless if either party had anything to say or not.

Dating outside of the school was rare, unless accompanied by an adult. However, if you had a local entertainment place in your town (such as a game room, bowling alley or skating rink), you could schedule a date by meeting each other at this location at the same time. It would still be considered a date, even if you arrived in separate cars.

The 'date' was rarely a one-on-one experience. It usually involved everyone's friends being there, too. Because of this, the guy and girl would have to act in a way towards each other that would be acceptable around their friends. A guy couldn't be sensitive towards his date because he risked the chance of getting punched by his friend standing next to him. This would show a sign of weakness for the male species and getting his man card revoked. Holding her hand would be acceptable because it showed how the female needed the male to keep her walking straight. Her desires for him would make her dizzy. He would keep her from tripping and falling down. Kissing her would be acceptable because this was considered 'first base'. Just like in baseball, you only had to go three more bases to get to home plate to score. It was all about getting that point for the man team.

Being A Young Man On The Job

After the high school days are over, everyone get older and gets jobs. It's the way it goes in life. If you were part of the fortunate kids, you got a few years extension added to high school called college. But, after a few years of that, you started working at a job, too.

Being a man on a job is a rewarding experience. You basically trade someone hours of your hard-earned labor for a monetary reward. The more money you make, the more manly you are as long as your job title fits the standards set forth by what men consider manly jobs. Here are some examples:

- Working at a fast food restaurant was considered an entry level manly job if you were the cook that flipped the hamburgers. If you ran the register, it was not.
- Men did not work at a florist because men shouldn't know anything about flowers. That was for the women. Flowers smell pretty and men should not.
- A construction worker was a manly job because it involved power tools, heavy machinery and using earthy products such as wood and cement. Construction workers were considered one with nature and this would make you very manly.
- A mechanic was a manly job because you worked on cars and trucks and got greasy. Women don't like grease, not

even on men. In addition, most women wouldn't be caught working on a vehicle, but they do like to drive one. A man with the ability to fix one would be considered very manly in the eyes of both men and women.

My first real job was a warehouse clerk. It was considered a manly job because we used box knives, opened boxes and drove forklifts. Even though women did the same job, we still considered it a manly job. I guess because opening a box with a knife was similar to gutting a fish and processing deer. We were ripping stuff open and yanking the insides out.

For the most part when I worked in the warehouse, male dominance wasn't obtained by fighting or spraying our man-scent on our territorial boundaries. Everybody worked together and shared the load. It was always a team effort. However, for us guys in the department, we competed for speed and quantity. We challenged each other to see who could do the most and do it the fastest. Every day was a game day to see who was the best. This also helped pass the time away so that we could go home. Sometimes we would hang out after work.

Being Social With The Fellas
After a rough day at work, sometimes a man needed to unwind. We would drive to the local pub to drink a few beers. We were

men and that's just what men did. Our fathers did it and so did their fathers before them. A real man drinks beer. However, a smart man knows his limits and keeps track of how many beers he drinks. He keeps his empty bottles at close visual range because he knew eventually he would have to drive home.

The place we would go to was down the road from where we worked. We would all pull up around the same time and go inside. Standing around with a beer bottle in your hand was the manly thing to do, so that's pretty much what we did the entire night. Some of us would play a game of pool, while the rest of us stood around and talked.

We were young and either in a relationship with a girlfriend or were looking for one. Most of our conversations seemed to center around women and what we expected out of one. Young guys have a certain image of what they want in a female. We think about important details such as height, hair and eye color and breast size. At this stage of life, we weren't concerned with the boring unnecessary stuff like "Can she cook?" or "Does she have a criminal background?" or "Is she mentally stable?". Those things weren't important yet.

We would talk about our jobs, but not the details of how we did them. It was mostly about the people that we worked with. Since we weren't at work, we could tell each other how we felt about certain people on the job. The snooty bosses, stressed out group leaders or the new girl they recently hired that looked super fine would make great topics to discuss.

The rest of the evening would include conversations about sports, cars and music. Unfortunately, these topics would cause division because some of us didn't really know much about them. I could talk all day about music, but as soon as someone started talking about sports or cars, I'm out. I wasn't a sports fan and didn't have a clue about cars. I would move on to the group that was talking about something I had in common.

After a few hours of hanging out together, everyone would drive home. I'm sure the ones that didn't monitor their drinking had a some difficulty getting there. We would know for sure the next day when we would see each other at work. The ones that didn't show up were probably hungover at home or parked in a ditch somewhere.

Being A Family Man

Changing The Mind Set
One thing I have learned about being a man with a wife and kids is that the world no longer revolves around me. It's no longer about the things I want out of life, but more about what 'we' can

do as a family. When you're a young dad, this way of thinking doesn't happen over night.

It's hard to go from being a young man, who is only concerned about himself, to a man that shares this life with his wife. Then, in a few years, he now has to share it with kids that bare his name. This is a big change and takes time to adapt.

A simple thing as going out on a date with your wife now involves more planning. You have to find a babysitter that's willing to watch your kids on a short notice. If you get lucky enough to find one, you have to make sure your child and the babysitter has everything they need while you're on your date. This involves packing their bag full of essentials. If you forget something, you will get a phone call and the date will be over. It can be frustrating.

Many times our date nights included our children. We would go to places where our kids could have fun, too. Bowling, watching a movie and having dinner would still be considered 'being on a date'. We just had to redefine what 'being on a date' meant for us.

There have been many times where my wife and I had a candlelit dinner prepared by us in the privacy of our own home. It would be after our kids had went to bed. At the time, I'm sure we were envious of how other couples could have real dates and we're stuck doing it at home. But, now that we are older and looking back, those dates were some of the best times of our lives.

I've heard guys talking about how they've lost a lot of friends when they got married and had children. They made it seem as though they now live in a miserable situation because they no longer have their old friends to hang out with. They're stuck with the family doing boring family things. Maybe they should have considered the 'family' as their 'new' choice of 'friends'.

I don't recall socializing with my old friends after I got married and had children. It's like my old friends disappeared. I would see them occasionally, but it would be at places like the County Fair, when it would come to town once a year, or when we went shopping. And when we would meet, I would notice that we had something in common. They had families, too. Maybe this was the new level of manhood called the 'family man', by being able to walk away from old friendships in order to build a longer lasting friendship with our spouse and children.

In my marriage, I do remember having guy friends that wanted to go and hang out. Most of these guys were either having marital problems at home or were divorced. People like this could stir up trouble in your marriage if you let them. Their lifestyle can become yours if you are hanging out with them and doing the same things. I've learned that they are like weeds that you have to remove. Being a man at this point in life is about stepping up to do the 'weeding' if you value your family. It's also about setting priorities and family being at the top of the list.

Learning to sacrifice is probably the hardest part of manhood. Having a family means putting aside things that you used to consider important. It can mean friendships. It could also be in the simple things such as what the family watches on television.

I LOVE YOU... YOU LOVE ME... WE'RE A HAPPY FAMILY...

SHAMSUNG HI-DEF

Yes, a man would like to watch an action movie with guts and blood spewing all over the TV screen. I'm sure it would be even better if it had hot babes in bikinis in every scene. To make the movie tougher, let every actor and actress talk trash by saying cuss words every 5 minutes. I mean, that would be cool. Right? But, would you want your 3 year old son watching it knowing that they could repeat every word? Or how how about this? Would you want them watching 'you' watch this? Now that's something to think about.

Making sacrifices to protect our families seems to be one of the main jobs of a man. For most of us, we're cool with working every day to financially support them. We're also cool with doing what we call the manly duties around the home. This is the manly stuff like cutting the grass, doing the home repairs, tackling the honey-do lists, working on the cars and even carrying the wife's shopping bags in when she returns from town spending our money. Right? For the most part, we're down with that. We're good. But, what about the other stuff?

Sometimes we are called to do the impossible – the women's stuff. This would include duties such as caring for our kids, washing clothes and dishes, cleaning the house and possibly cooking dinner. Holy cow! That's a forbidden zone! Right? It's not in our DNA. We weren't wired for this. But, what if?

People get sick. This would include our wives, too. Would you be willing to step in and fill her shoes during her down time? We said we would according to our wedding vows. Being a man would mean sticking to our word. Learning to use a vacuum cleaner would be a good start. Sometimes you have to think about the condition of your home when the main caretaker isn't available. If your wife is sick, it makes sense to step up and do it. Who else is going to do it? And who's to say that cleaning the home is her job anyway? What if marriage was just another word for teamwork? It could basically mean a man and woman working together towards the same goal by sharing the full load together. A system like that could create peace and harmony. Nobody would get stressed because they could lean on each other to get the job done. Being a man would mean working together with the one we love for the sake of the family and the home.

I know in my house, my wife and I both work. Actually, we work in a business that we both own and we work together. I can't say that my job is more important than hers because she does the same things that I do in our business together. I can't come home from a tired day at work and prop up in my recliner while she cleans house and prepares dinner. She's just as tired as I am. It wouldn't be fair. How do we make our life together peaceful? We continue to do everything together after business hours.

She and I will tackle the house as a team by cleaning, vacuuming, cooking dinner and tending to the kids. Since two people are working together, the time it takes to do the job is cut in half. We both can stop at the same time and sit down together to relax and watch TV. Our communication is better because we are usually in the same room doing the same things. Our life is peaceful because it flows better.

Does is make me less of a man because I do laundry? Or does it make me more of a man because I work with my life partner on all home duties as team? It takes guts to step up and do what the world considers a 'woman's job'.

I hate shopping. I think it's silly to waste countless hours looking at stuff in a store, especially things you don't need. If you don't need it, don't look at it. If you look at it too long, you'll convince yourself that you need it. Then you'll buy it. It's basic economics. If you're broke, the safest place for you is to stay at home. If I need something, I'll tell my wife and she will go to the store to get it. My wife likes to shop. She has frequent flier miles at the local Wally World. They know her by name.

Last night after work, I cleaned house while she went shopping for groceries. Both activities are productive and required – we get food for the family and we get a clean house at the same time. By splitting up as a team and tackling both tasks, we both get a free peaceful weekend to do whatever we please. Everyone is happy.

Did I break a man code? Probably, according to the world. Did it affect my manhood? Not at all.

Men
The Role Models To Our Children

I believe our kids watch us. They watch how we live our life and how we treat others. They learn from us and could possibly turn out to be like us as adults. Are we being good examples?

Our kids already have enough influence in the world to help them become men. They can learn from other men figures. They can learn from their choice of friends that have been influenced by men figures. I believe what they truly need is a good influence from their own fathers.

It's sad and I know from experience that some men choose to bail out. They would rather remove themselves from their child's life and let others do their job for them. It's a wimpy approach, but the reality is that many men in the world are doing it. Their kids will go through life without them leading the way. They won't be the role models for them that they were intended to be. It's a sad loss for the both of them.

As men, we have a big job. I believe one of those jobs is being role models to our children and being there for them. I know that how we act around them originated from the things we learned from other men when we were kids. Those things that we were taught could be the reason we act the way we do today. There comes a point when we have to determine if what we learned is actually good traits to have because, believe it or not, we're fixing to share the example with our kids that are now watching us. Do we pass the torch that we carry? Or do we blow out the flame and start over with a new and improved one?

If we know that the things we do creates negativity in our kids, we should stop doing it. Back in the days when I worked in Corporate America, I would get really stressed from work. I worked there to improve my family's way of life. I wanted them to have better and nicer things. And that's OK, but for me it came with a price. Stress is a terrible thing. It would be good if a person could leave their stress at work, but it's hard and many times we bring it home. I learned that the way to combat this stress at home was to add alcohol to it. A few beers a days keeps the stress away. Right? Unfortunately, beer relaxes the mind sometimes to the point to where you can't hear the world around you. The sweet voices of our little children wanting to spend time with us becomes a faint sound of nothingness.

Sometimes you no longer realize they are in the same room. Eventually, they will feel neglected and won't even know who you are anymore. Is this the male role model we want them to see? Yeah, me neither.

Changes have to be made. There's a chance that our kids will turn out to be like us or will marry someone like us. For some of us, that's a scary thought. Hopefully, they can separate our good and bad traits that they have seen in us and do something positive with their own life. Or maybe we can make those changes while there is still time.

Just remember, if we don't set the example of a man to our kids, the world will. The world will be more than happy to fill your position as their father. Do you want to be replaced?

The World's Reflection
Of A Man

Media – A Source For Manhood

The world has it's way of raising our kids when we aren't available. When it comes to being a man, the world offers its own interpretation and will gladly share them with us. Media provides many examples of men and how they should properly act. Our kids watch them every day on television and on the internet and take mental notes. The reality is that we are all human and we will make mistakes in life. Idolizing people in the spotlight can leave us feeling empty when their bright light dims. Here are some examples:

A professional golfer, who achieves worldly success through hard work and determination, wins approval as a role model to a generation. Kids look up to him and want to be like him when they grow up. But then, we discover that his life wasn't so perfect. We learn that he cheats on his wife and gets arrested for DUI. A major let down.

An Olympic winner, who achieved success by overcoming adversity, becomes known to the world as 'an all-American hero' and 'world's greatest athlete'. He was a man that everyone looked up to. Actually, they put his athletic image on a cereal box for the kids to look at every morning. He was the perfect definition of what a man should and can be. Years later, he decides to change his image and become a woman. The world is devastated.

Musical artists have always touched our lives through their music. We have connected with them through their lyrics and their lifestyles. We have changed our clothing styles and personalities to match theirs. Later, as their popularity fades, we learn that they were just another criminal with years of drug abuse and serious moral issues.

I had a few bands that I admired as a child. MTV (Music Television) made them cool and gave them a tough image. Their music was awesome and helped define who I was as a teen. I guess something changes when you get older and you look at people from a different eye view. Thirty years later, I got a chance to meet one of those favorite singers of mine at a convention in Atlanta. Yes, he had aged, but he basically looked the same as I remembered. He still had that tough image. I guess I expected him to say something cool as I stood in front of him with my star-glazed look in my eyes. Maybe I expected him to throw a rock symbol in the air with his hands and say, "The 80's rocked!" or "Long live Rock-n-Roll!"

But, no. Instead, he looked lost and all he said was, "Uhh... I need a cigarette." This was a major let down. I walked away feeling very sad. This super star from my youth no longer shined. I guess I expected too much.

The reality is that this person is a human. He was a human back in the day, too. Media just made him look superhuman through the eyes of a teenager. They sold music and merchandise by presenting a man with a band that would appeal to my generation. And it worked. But, it was all an act for the sake of money.

Stars of the TV screen are no different. They are actors - people wearing masks – that entertain us. They get paid to be who we want them to be. If we idolize them, they set the stage for failure when they remove their masks in the real world. This is when we see the real picture of who they really are – human.

It's not only kids that are influenced by media. I think everyone one is – all age groups. When it comes to defining what a man is, we look to media to tell us.

A commercial comes on TV and says, "Brand X Cologne is made for real men. One spray and the women go wild." Next thing you know, boys and men are wanting this cologne for Christmas. The product guarantees that, by wearing it, we will attract the ladies. We buy into it and learn that it doesn't work like that in the real world. Yes, we may smell better, but where are those ladies? Don't worry. They are out there shopping for that product that media told them to buy, too. You know, the one that would help them remove wrinkles, look younger and have that irresistible aroma that will attract more men.

If a company can put a famous male celebrity's face on their product, men will buy it. And if the men don't buy it, their wives will. Why? Because everyone wants to be like the one they subconsciously idolize. For the men, take a look at most things you buy. Chances are, it's endorsed by a famous male person or a hot looking female that probably doesn't have a clue as to what the product is or how it works. It's all money-driven. To sell a product, a company has to pay big advertisement bucks to attract their desired audience.

Think about this. If you're like me, 50% of your wardrobe consists of clothes that look like trees. Camouflage is manly – no doubt. It tells the world that you are a man that is in tune with nature. It defines you as a hunter, a sportsmen and all that is manly. If you were to go out and hang with other men in a group, the first thing you would grab from your closet would be camouflaged – shirt, pants, boots and cap. The funny thing is that some of the men that wear this have never hunted a day in their life. But, it defines a man. Why? I'm sure media had something to do with it. Would our grandparents wear a tree-printed t-shirt a hundred years ago? Of course not. That would have been silly. Media, at that time, told them to wear three-piece suits with a top hat – while sporting wide curly mustaches.

Sometimes companies create an audience by making people feel like they should be part of this new trend. By making their product 'trendy', people will change their appearance in order to fit in. Here's a good example: the man bun. Men basically grow their hair long and roll it up into a bun on top of their head. This is same hair bun that many of the older ladies had back in the old days. It may not seem like a big deal, but because of this new hairstyle, companies are now able to sell more hair products and accessories. Not only are their customers women, but now they added a population of trendy men that want to be part of the scene. It's not that having a man bun is a bad thing, but it's kinda funny how a man will proudly sport a hairdo that he knows his grandfather would have disapproved of when he was their age. All because media made it popular.

For my generation now, it is normal for men to lose their hair. I mean, that's life. So what! Back in the 70's, a fashionable man would simply grow it long on the sides and comb it over the top. It was sleek and debonair. The ladies loved it. But now, the comb over is considered old fashioned. The new look for men is for them to simply shave their heads bald. It's a simple do-it-yourself project that looks extra fashionable with a big burly beard. That's the new man look. Here's the money exchange. The sales of buzz cutters, razors and beard trimmers went up. Now you have a whole row of hair products for men at your local Wally World. Who started this trend? I'm sure media had something to do with it.

What's the top-selling soft drink among the men in America? It's Coca-Cola. Did you know that they sponsor a lot of the cool entertainment we watch on TV? NASCAR, NBA, NCAA are just a few. By knowing what men watch on television, a company can spend money to sponsor it. In turn, you get to watch their advertisements and will probably buy their product because it is presented as a product for the men. Pretty cool, huh?

Media is a powerful tool. And because of the money that companies pour into it, it becomes a tool to manipulate people and define them.

- When does a man know when it's time for a hairstyle change?
- When does he know when it's time to change his complete wardrobe?
- Who said that men can't be sensitive to their wives?
- How can one decade of men wear pink shirts while men a few decades later can't?
- Who said men can't cry at a movie?
- Who said that real men drive trucks and that a minivan was a woman's car?

Could all of this have some media influence? Could it be from what we watch on television or our computers – from movies, commercials and other forms of advertisement? Are we allowing media to tell us 'what it means to be a man'? Probably.

There's something I have noticed in the news within the past year. There seems to be an identity crisis. Men want to use female restrooms and women want to use men's restrooms in public places. This wouldn't be a problem if there were just one toilet in a bathroom with a door lock, but for a man to want to poop beside a woman in the next stall just seems weird. It's all fun and games when you do this to your wife at home when she's brushing her teeth, but I don't see this being a good thing in public. In all honesty, do women really

73

want to share a bathroom with a guy? And what about bathroom etiquette? Will men be required to lift the lid when they pee and lower it when they're finished? Will women push the issue of mandatory matching bathroom rugs and accessories in the stalls? There could be some problems.

I read lately that an organization that, for many years was exclusively for boys, is being targeted by feminists. This organization has had the reputation of training young boys to become men, but now it seems that Boys Scouts Of America will be taking female members into their group. What's that all about? It's called 'boy' scouts for a reason - it's for boys. Girl Scouts is for girls. I can understand if they created an organization called The Scouts of America that enlisted both girls and boys. They could build campfires and tie knots together. That would be a good thing and could be beneficial in the real world. It seems like a person's gender is being torn down and redefined.

I can remember a few years back signing my daughter up for baseball. She was on a team with all boys. I thought this was cool because I felt she was just as good as any of the other players on the team. She could show the boys how good a girl baseball player could be. I was a proud Dad, but there was a problem. My daughter also liked to dance and enjoyed displaying her skills on the ball field during the games. It was cute and the audience smiled. That was, until the boys followed along with her and started dancing, too. My daughter had transformed these tough looking ball players into delicate ballet performers. The whole outfield was performing Swan Lake as the balls rolled passed them. No wonder they didn't win any games.

Maybe the world is changing. Fifty years ago, it was common for the man to protect and financially support his family by himself. The wife's primary role was in the home raising the children. But, these days it's not like that anymore. Both genders work and share the workload. Economically speaking, it costs more to live and requires more than one income for the family. Maybe this economy is the reason for all of these new changes. We're learning to adapt in each others playing field. The hard part is to be willing to conform because our mindset is in the 1950's. Maybe redefining 'what a man should be' will lower the current 50% failure rate of marriages.

In my marriage, I have always been the main financial provider. It's not that I was the only one working. It was because I made the most. There's a lot of pride that can build up when you know you 'bring home 75% of the bacon'. But, it's an expected feeling for a man that grew up knowing that men were supposed to be the bread winners for the home. It's what we do.

Ten years ago was a rough time for a lot of people in America. The real estate crisis caused a lot of men to be out of work. Many of them were forced to stay home. It was hard to find a job. That's how it was for me, too. I had worked in construction in my own business. As soon as the economy tanked, I was the first one to get hit. I was helpless and couldn't do anything about it. I tried searching for work. It just wasn't out there. My wife, however, found a job as a nanny. She was now the sole bread winner of our home and we exchanged roles.

I got the kids dressed for school. I cleaned the house and cooked dinner. I did everything that she used to do. This went on for a couple of years. Can you imagine how this would feel knowing that you were supposed to be the man of the house, but doing a woman's job? This will tear you down mentally. Any pride you may have had as a man is now gone. You would definitely want to keep this secret to yourself when you are around your male friends.

"Hey, Steve. How are you?"

"Oh, not too bad. Just another busy day at the office. How about yourself?"

"Aww, man. Let me tell ya. I had a lot of laundry to do today. It was just piled up to the ceiling. Those crazy kids of mine sure do make big messes. It took me forever to get the house cleaned up... and that little Johnny spilled the whole dang bowl of Spaghetti-O's on the floor that I made him for lunch. I sure hope the wife is happy with how the house looks when she gets home from work. Wanna go fishing later?"

"Umm... yeah. Not today. Gotta run. Good to see ya."

Now that I look back on my experience, I can honestly say that I learned a lot. I learned to appreciate my wife more. All these years before, she had been doing this without complaining. I learned that, as a man, I could do a woman's job. Actually, I got really good at it. My wife never came home to a dirty house. I learned that housework is a job that seems to go unnoticed by people that only consider their paying job a 'real' job. This experience has redefined me as a man.

On the flip side, being the only one working, this experience has redefined my wife, too. She now knows what it was like for me being a man. Now we can take what we've learned and work together – becoming stronger and better than before.

With all of the influences I've had growing up in life, how did I turn out? Let's just say that I am not the man I used to be. I am still a work in progress. I decided years ago that the direction I was taking my life wasn't in a positive direction. I needed help and chose to reach out to the Lord to guide and direct me.

I have learned that His ways are better and that He has a purpose for me. The training is continuous and there is always something new for me to learn. To be a man, I have to learn from the man. His name is Jesus.

God's Reflection Of A Man

Man – An Image Of God

And God said, Let us make man in our image - Genesis 1: 26

To learn more about being a man, you have to start at the beginning. As many of us already know, the creation of man begins in the first book of the Bible - in Genesis. The very first man was Adam. I'm sure you have heard of him. He was created on the last day after everything else was created – the stars, the Earth, trees, animals, water, etc. – in the image and likeness of God.

The Bible tells us that Adam was formed by God from dust and He gave him life by sharing His own breath. It says He breathed life into his nostrils and he became a living soul.

And the Lord God formed man of the dust of the ground, and breathed into his nostrils the breath of life; and man became a living soul. - Genesis 2: 7

Out of all of God's creations, humanity is different. We have both a physical body and a soul. God is spirit and exists without a body.

God is a Spirit: and they that worship him must worship him in spirit and in truth. - John 4: 24

Adam was created in the likeness of God by having perfect health and not having to worry about death. God also gave him dominion over the Earth. He was in charge of it all.

And God blessed them, and God said unto them, Be fruitful, and multiply, and replenish the earth, and subdue it: and have dominion over the fish of the sea, and over the fowl of the air, and over every living thing that moveth upon the earth. - Genesis 1: 28

This separates human beings from the animal world because we can talk with God on a personal level. We share the likeness of God mentally, morally and socially.

Mentally, as human beings created by God, we are given the ability to reason and make choices. This is a reflection of God's intellect and freedom. Anytime someone writes a book, enjoys a song, paints a picture or invents something, they are sharing the fact that we are made in God's image.

Morally, human beings were created in righteousness and perfect innocence, which is a reflection of God's holiness. When God saw all that he created, including humans, He called it 'very good'.

And God saw every thing that he had made, and, behold, it was very good. - Genesis 1: 31a

Our conscience is a reminder of that original state. When we refuse to do something wrong or we recognize a good deed, it is a confirmation that we are created in the likeness of God.

Socially, humans were created to have relationships with one another. In the Garden of Eden, Adam and Eve had a relationship with God.

And they heard the voice of the Lord God walking in the garden in the cool of the day: and Adam and his wife hid themselves from the presence of the Lord God amongst the trees of the garden. - Genesis 3: 8

God created Eve so that Adam would not be alone.

And the Lord God said, It is not good that the man should be alone; I will make him an help meet for him. - Genesis 2: 18

Every time a couple gets married, a person makes a friend or hugs one another, they are reflecting that they are made in the likeness of God.

Part of being made in God's image was that Adam was able to have freedom of choice. Even though both Adam and Eve were given a righteous nature, they made the choice to rebel against God. When they did, they distorted His image and passed this damaged likeness on to their descendants.

Wherefore, as by one man sin entered into the world, and death by sin; and so death passed upon all men, for that all have sinned: - Romans 5: 12

Even today, we still have the image of God, but we also bear the the scars of sin. Mentally, morally, socially and physically, we show the effects of sin.

The good news is that when God redeems a person, He begins restoring the original image of God, creating a 'new person' to be like God in righteousness and holiness.

And that ye put on the new man, which after God is created in righteousness and true holiness. - Ephesians 4: 24

This redemption is only available by God's grace through Jesus Christ – our Savior from the sin that separates us from God.

For by grace are ye saved through faith; and that not of yourselves: it is the gift of God: Not of works, lest any man should boast. - Ephesians 2: 8, 9

Through Jesus, we are made 'new creations' in the likeness of God.

For we know that if our earthly house of this tabernacle were dissolved, we have a building of God, an house not made with hands, eternal in the heavens. For in this we groan, earnestly desiring to be clothed upon with our house which is from heaven: If so be that being clothed we shall not be found naked. For we that are in this tabernacle do groan, being burdened: not for that we would be unclothed, but clothed upon, that mortality might be swallowed up of life. Now he that hath wrought us for the selfsame thing is God, who also hath given unto us the earnest of the Spirit. Therefore we are always confident, knowing that, whilst we are at home in the body, we are absent from the Lord: (For we walk by faith, not by sight:) - 2 Corinthians 5: 1-7

Jesus – The Example Of Being A Man
Because of the destruction created by sin, God sent Jesus to restore humanity.

For God so loved the world, that he gave his only begotten Son, that whosoever believeth in him should not perish, but have everlasting life. - John 3: 16

Not only does Jesus save us from our sins, He provides us with the perfect example of how we should be. The way He lived His life here on Earth should be the way we should live ours. For the men, He is our role model for manhood that we can read about from the Bible. What could we learn from Him?

Jesus was full of the Holy Spirit and was dependent and obedient to the will of God. Basically, He did what God told Him to do and relied on Him to make it happen. That's how we should live our lives, too.

We should do this by studying God's Word and applying it – putting it into practice every day in the way we act and conduct ourselves when we are around others. As a man of God, we are to be a reflection of Jesus. Jesus displayed the fruits of the Spirit that are mentioned in Galatians. I believe a 'true' man will reflect these works of the Spirit, too.

But the fruit of the Spirit is love, joy, peace, longsuffering, gentleness, goodness, faith, meekness, temperance: against such there is no law. - Galatians 5: 22-23

Love
And we have known and believed the love that God hath to us. God is love; and he that dwelleth in love dwelleth in God, and God in him. - 1 John 4: 16

Through Jesus Christ, our greatest goal as a man is to do all things in love. Our thoughts and actions should reflect love. Do you know what it means to love? I'm not talking about the puppy love you had when you were in elementary school. Boy meets girl, they exchange a couple of letters and boom – instant love.

Sorry folks, this kind of love doesn't last. What type of love did Jesus have? Love is explained in 1 Corithians:

Charity suffereth long, and is kind; charity envieth not; charity vaunteth not itself, is not puffed up, Doth not behave itself unseemly, seeketh not her own, is not easily provoked, thinketh no evil; Rejoiceth not in iniquity, but rejoiceth in the truth; Beareth all things, believeth all things, hopeth all things, endureth all things. Charity never faileth: but whether there be prophecies, they shall fail; whether there be tongues, they shall cease; whether there be knowledge, it shall vanish away. - 1 Corinthians 13: 4-8

Verses 4 through 8 from 1 Corinthians gives us examples of what love (charity) is:

- Love is patient
- Love is kind
- Love doesn't envy
- Love doesn't boast
- Love isn't proud
- Love isn't rude
- Love isn't self-seeking
- Love isn't easily angered
- Love doesn't keep records of wrong
- Love doesn't delight in evil
- Love rejoices with the truth
- Love always protects
- Love always trusts
- Love always hopes
- Love always perseveres
- Love never fails

When you say you love someone, whether it be your wife, kids or family and friends, check your love against this list to make sure it qualifies as true love – the kind of love that Jesus had.

Joy

...for the joy of the Lord is your strength. - Nehemiah 8: 10b

Looking unto Jesus the author and finisher of our faith; who for the joy that was set before him endured the cross, despising the shame, and is set down at the right hand of the throne of God. - Hebrews 12: 2

Joy is the emotion of great delight or happiness caused by something exceptionally good or satisfying. Joy gives spiritual strength. To put it plainly, God wants us to be happy and joy is a fruit of the Spirit. As men that serve God, we should be happy people that smile. We can't walk around being grumpy all the time with frowns on our faces. Jesus was a happy person and so should we.

When we face problems in life, we should continue to be happy because we know the Lord is in control. We reflect that when we continue to be happy people even though things around us seem to be going wrong.

A real mood changer for me is car problems. I could be in a good mood all week – laughing, telling jokes and smiling. But, if one of my cars decides to break down, my normal reaction is to frown. I'm not a mechanic and I get stressed. I know this repair will cost me money and most of the time I don't have the skills to repair it myself. I also know that one vehicle is for the family and the other one is for work. A broken vehicle will either affect the family life or will put a halt to business that will, in turn, affect our income. Repairs have to be made quickly. As a man of God, I have to continue smiling and be joyful. As the mechanic is fixing my car and piling up debt on me, I still need to be joyful. Everything is in God's hands and will work it out for my good.

And we know that all things work together for good to them that love God, to them who are the called according to his purpose. - *Romans 8: 28*

Peace

Therefore being justified by faith, we have peace with God through our Lord Jesus Christ: - Romans 5: 1

Now the God of hope fill you with all joy and peace in believing, that ye may abound in hope, through the power of the Holy Ghost. - Romans 15: 13

There is peace when we are serving God. Just like joy, we should have peace because we know that God has our life in His hands. When we face storms in life, we should take a moment to breathe and thank God for His assurance from His Word.

As leaders of our home, we can relax and not feel that we are taking on the full load in life. God is there with us through everything that we face. He is leading us so that we can lead our families. We're not alone.

Longsuffering

Longsuffering means having or showing patience in spite of troubles, especially those caused by other people.

Strengthened with all might, according to his glorious power, unto all patience and longsuffering with joyfulness; - Colossians 1: 11

With all lowliness and meekness, with longsuffering, forbearing one another in love; - Ephesians 4: 2

Who has patience? Especially when it comes to dealing with certain people? I'm normally a patient person. My kids are the ones that sometimes get on my nerves. They can be irritating, hard-headed and they know how to pull my strings. Now that I'm older, I have learned to be more patient around them. I understand that they get this trait from their mother. So, instead of snapping on them, I have learned to be more sympathetic and actually feel sorry for the little heathens.

My wife, on the other hand, is quick to snap on anybody. It could be the kids or it could be the people in their cars on the busy expressway. It don't take much to pull her string. It's probably because of her age and the whole menopause thing. I know that women go through changes in life and snapping the necks of innocent people is just part of that change. It's all good and I will always be there by her side to calm her down.

Jesus was a patient man. As God continues to work in our lives, we will develop this fruit of the Spirit, too. For some of us, it may take a while.

Gentleness

Gentleness means being kind and having the absence of harshness or severity. As men, we should live:

By pureness, by knowledge, by long suffering, by kindness, by the Holy Ghost, by love unfeigned, by the word of truth, by the power of God, by the armour of righteousness on the right hand and on the left, - 2 Corinthians 6: 6-7

In today's world, being a 'gentle' man (not gentleman) will probably get your man card revoked. The world teaches us that real men are rough and tough. If you're not, you might as well wear Capri pants, put on some makeup and hang out with the ladies.

But here in the Bible, being gentle is a good trait to have. Jesus was a gentle man. He was kind to others and sensitive to people's needs. He actually cared about people. If we are to live like Jesus, we probably should start hugging folks.

Goodness

Wherefore also we pray always for you, that our God would count you worthy of this calling, and fulfil all the good pleasure of his goodness, and the work of faith with power: - 2 Thessalonians 1:11

92

For the fruit of the Spirit is in all goodness and righteousness and truth; - Ephesians 5:9

There are some good people in this world. There may not be as many as they were several years ago, but they do exist. I have met some of them. These are the people that care about you and offer to help you in your time of need. I am thankful for them.

As men living by the Bible, we are to be good people, too. This would involve thinking about others and not ourselves. We can no longer be self-centered. Being this way may have been cool when we were kids, but now that we are men reflecting Jesus, we have to reach out to people and do good things for them. We shouldn't expect anything in return.

An example of 'being good' to me is when I see people opening doors for others. It's a simple gesture that packs a lot of power. It lets me know that there is still good in the world and the fact that this person was raised correctly. I imagine if doors were invented back when Jesus walked the Earth, He would have opened them for us, too.

Faith
O Lord, thou art my God; I will exalt thee, I will praise thy name; for thou hast done wonderful things; thy counsels of old are

faithfulness and truth. - Isaiah 25: 1

That he would grant you, according to the riches of his glory, to be strengthened with might by his Spirit in the inner man; that Christ may dwell in your hearts by faith; that ye, being rooted and grounded in love, - Ephesians 3: 16-17

Faith is simply trusting that God is who He says He is and we trust the Bible as truth. The world is full of beliefs that go in a totally different direction. As men living for God, we need to make sure we are rooted in our faith in Him.

If you need some examples of people that had faith, read Hebrews 11. These folks stood the tests and remained faithful to God. And we should, too.

Meekness

Brethren, if a man be overtaken in a fault, ye which are spiritual, restore such an one in the spirit of meekness; considering thyself, lest thou also be tempted. - Galatians 6: 1

With all lowliness and meekness, with longsuffering, forbearing one another in love; - Ephesians 4: 2

The world's definition of being meek is that of a wimpy spineless person. This is the kind of person that you could easily walk on and take advantage of. The Bible's meaning is different. Meakness is not weakness. Meekness is simply ME getting out of my life's equation, so that Jesus can be ALL in ALL – that should be the goal of every Christian.

MEEK

MEEK IS GOOD.

ARG READERS

No matter what goes on in your life, being meek means realizing that God is in control. If we're meek, pride and arrogance about ourselves should be missing. We are totally dependent upon God for everything. By being this way, we are more teachable and usable for God's service to others.

Take my yoke upon you, and learn of me; for I am meek and lowly in heart: and ye shall find rest unto your souls. - Matthew 11: 29

Jesus was meek. Even though He was King of kings and Lord of lords, He could have entered Jerusalem on a strong white stallion, but instead he chose a donkey. He was meek enough to spend time with others; the sick and dying, the blind and deaf, and those the world considered 'lower class'. Jesus had surrendered His life to the will of God.

Temperance
And beside this, giving all diligence, add to your faith virtue; and to virtue knowledge; and to knowledge temperance; and to temperance patience; and to patience godliness; and to godliness

brotherly kindness; and to brotherly kindness charity. - 2 Peter 1: 5-7

Having temperance simply means having self control. It's the ability to say 'no' to our fleshly lusts and desires. It's knowing when we've had enough at the dinner table and putting the fork down. It's the ability to walk away from things that could cause you harm or trouble. It's being able to walk away from clearance sales because we realize that we don't actually need the items being sold at such a discounted price. Uh oh!

My wife is going to beat me up about this, but she has always loved shopping. I will admit that she has changed through the years. There was a time when she could buy pretty much what she wanted. Then, the economy crashed in 2008, and we were too broke to spend a dime. The lessons she learned during that time has created a very 'temperant' person. She no longer spends money like she used to. Now she is very frugal and only buys what's on the clearance racks or at the local thrift stores, whether we need the stuff or not. She has developed self control in the way she spends money. It's no longer about just buying the fad. It's now a mission to get it at rock bottom prices. She, too, is a work in progress.

Characteristics Of Jesus For Men To Follow

We live in a world where a person's image is important. It's their looks and the clothes they wear that defines them. We use this outward appearance to judge their character without really getting to know them on a personal level. We make assumptions about them by their appearance only. That's sad.

I remember shopping with my wife one day. It was cold outside, so I decided to wear a thick Army jacket. I'll admit, I'm not a fashionable guy. I mostly wear t-shirts, blue jeans and my old ball cap – nothing fancy. My face wasn't shaven. I don't try to impress people, so I usually dress how I want to when I go out in public. My wife has given up on trying to change me. It's just how I am.

We were out of town and my wife decides she wants to shop at their local Goodwill. I went inside with her and looked around. Usually if I don't find anything I'm interested in within 15 minutes, I'll go sit down somewhere while she does her shopping. I walked around the aisles, looked at the outdated electronics and didn't find anything, so I found a cozy little sofa. I sat down and got relaxed. The next thing I know, a store manager walks up to me.

"Excuse me, sir. You're gonna have to get up."

"What? What's wrong?"

"You can't sit on the sofas."

So I get up and was a little upset. I could be wrong, but I felt like the man thought I may have been a homeless bum looking for a place to sleep. I went to find my wife and told her to leave her buggy. I wanted to leave. So we did.

Maybe their store has a 'no sitting on our stuff' policy and I just blew it out of proportion. But then, I sit on the sofas all the time at our Goodwill in our hometown. Or maybe they get a lot of homeless people coming in their store to find comfort from being out in the cold. I mean, I did look a little different with my big Army jacket and my homely-looking attire. I could have looked like a homeless man to him. Who knows?

The Bible doesn't put a lot of detail in telling us what Jesus looks like. From what I've read, the people were expecting their Savior to be a fancy King and what they got was a poor carpenter's kid. Most of what we read about Jesus is His characteristics – His character traits. I believe it was done on purpose so that we would be more concerned with how he acted instead of how he looked. We can follow what we learn about Him from the Bible, and apply it to our life, to become more like Him.

Obedient To The Will Of God

Then said he, Lo, I come to do thy will, O God. He taketh away the first, that he may establish the second. - Hebrews 10: 9

Jesus was here to do the will of God. Period. God had a plan. He sent Jesus to get it done. And that's what Jesus did.

As men living for the Lord, that should be our purpose and mission, too. We should be about our Heavenly Father's business.

And He said to them,"Why did you seek Me? Did you not know that I must be about My Father's business?" - Luke 2: 49

What is it that God is telling you to do? What skills and talents do you have? Has the Lord blessed you with something? These are probably the tools that He has given you to use to serve Him.

He Will Endure Opposition And Never Lose Heart

For consider him that endured such contradiction of sinners against himself, lest ye be wearied and faint in your minds. - Hebrews 12: 3

Jesus had to face a lot of people that didn't really like what He was all about. They didn't want to hear His words or see His face. They didn't like Him. They didn't realize He was there to save them.

Yeah, Jesus could have taken it personally and got upset. He could have been sensitive and just gave up. He could have prayed:

"Dear Father in Heaven, I know you sent me here to save these folks, but some of these mean people are hurting my feelings. Every time I turn around, people are calling me names and doing all kinds of crazy stuff. It's hard to do your will with these folks messing with me. Let's just abort the mission. Can we? Just take me back home and let them figure it out. They seem like they know it all anyway. Amen?"

But, He didn't. He endured to the end.

That's how we should be when we face obstacles in life. Pray about it and let God handle it. Endure the situation until God provides the solution.

Be A Man Of The Word - Overcome Temptation

The verses from Matthew 4: 1-11 contain scripture that talks about the temptations that Jesus had to face. Satan tempted Him with three things after He had fasted for forty days. In all three accounts, Jesus used scripture to overcome those temptations. These are temptations that we will face in our life based on their category:

Physical Temptation: Do What Feels Right

Emotional Temptation: Question God's Love

Control Temptation: Take Over The Throne

We should do like Jesus did and use scripture to help us overcome temptations. Use the Bible as a tool to defeat the enemy when he tempts you with your weaknesses. It's best to read your Bible, learn scriptures and make it a regular practice in your life. The Bible is more than a great literary work. It's part of your arsenal as a soldier of God.

Be A Man Of Prayer

And in the morning, rising up a great while before day, he went out, and departed into a solitary place, and there prayed. - Mark 1: 35

Prayer is how we communicate with God. The interesting thing from this scripture is that Jesus prayed early in the morning. I don't know about you, but I mostly pray at night right before bedtime. I guess many of us think that it really doesn't matter when you pray as long as you pray. That's probably right.

But, what would be the importance of Jesus praying early in the morning? Around my house, early in the morning is the quietest time of the day. If you have children you'll know what I mean. If you're going to get anything done, it's best to do it before the noise-makers wake up. Am I right?

BUTT CRACK O'DAWN

After a busy day, you get kinda tired. You come home and relax. It seems the darker it gets outside the more sleepier you get. You know it's bedtime when you can barely keep your eyes open. It's like your body shuts down. The interesting thing is that it's also the time when many people decide to pray. I'm guilty of it, too. We wait until our brain is too tired to think before we decide to communicate with God through prayer. I have fell asleep before while praying. That's not good. Maybe Jesus chose early morning prayer because He knew that He would be wide awake and alert. Maybe He knew that communication with God was important and chose to do it first thing in the morning, instead of the last. That would make good sense.

As men of God, we should make prayer a priority in our life.

Be A Man Of Love And Sacrifice

Now before the feast of the passover, when Jesus knew that his hour was come that he should depart out of this world unto the Father, having loved his own which were in the world, he loved them unto the end. - John 13: 1

Jesus loved people. Actually, He loved them so much that He died for them. That's a big sacrifice.

LOVE = SACRIFICE

ARG READERS

I love people, too. But, I can't think of too many of them that I would be willing to die for - well, maybe my wife and kids, my mother and my grandbabies. That's pretty much it.

Maybe the keyword in loving people is the word 'sacrifice'. There are things we could sacrifice that doesn't involve death. Our time and possessions are things we hold dear, but could we sacrifice them out of love for people? Possibly.

A person's car breaks down in the middle of the road. You don't know this person, but they need some help. Could you sacrifice your time by helping them push the car out of the way? What if it was hot outside? Some people would.

A homeless person asks you for some spare change so that they could buy some food to eat. Would you give it to them? It's debatable. I think some people would more than likely go buy the food first and give it to them instead.

It's situations like this that gives us a chance to demonstrate our character. To be a man of God, we could ask ourselves, "What would Jesus do?" The answer could determine if we are really living the life that He would have us to live, especially when our normal response is different.

Humble service
He riseth from supper, and laid aside his garments; and took a towel, and girded himself. After that he poureth water into a bason, and began to wash the disciples' feet, and to wipe them with the towel wherewith he was girded. - John 13: 4, 5

Jesus washed the disciples' feet. Eww! That's kinda gross, but it shows His character as a humble servant.

I don't think I can wash someone's feet. Can you? I don't think I could even wash my wife's feet. Feet contain germs. Plus, they're ugly to look at and they smell. In order to wash someone's feet, you would have to squat down and touch them – with your hands. I think I would rather clean out a septic tank.

STINK B-GONE

ARG READERS

But, if we are to live our life like Jesus, we are to be humble enough to wash the little piggies from someone's feet. That could be a life-changing experience. But, maybe that's what it all about.

Holiness

But as he which hath called you is holy, so be ye holy in all manner of conversation; because it is written, Be ye holy; for I am holy. - 1 Peter 1: 15-16

Holy in conversation? This is about how we talk to others.

I have heard that whatever comes out of our mouths reflects what's in our hearts. If we truly honor God, then the words that come out will also honor Him as we have conversations with people.

If we are constantly talking bad about people with our friends, maybe this would not be a good thing. Jesus loves people. He spent His life here building people up – not putting them down.

If we tell stories that are not true, this way of communicating goes against God. He is all about truth (read John 14: 6). Lying to someone is actually a bad thing.

Lie not one to another, seeing that ye have put off the old man with his deeds - Colossians 3: 9

The use of cuss words may not be good when talking with others. I mean, they do sound cool and all, but are they necessary? I have a hard time imagining Jesus talking this way. Do you?

Let no corrupt communication proceed out of your mouth, but that which is good to the use of edifying, that it may minister grace unto the hearers. - Ephesians 4: 29

As men trying to reflect the image of Jesus in our life, choosing our words wisely would be a good attribute – especially when we are talking to people.

Righteousness
Little children, let no man deceive you: he that doeth righteousness is righteous, even as he is righteous. - I John 3: 7

Jesus was a righteous man. That simply means that He had good morals. The Bible is the standard we should go by for achieving human righteousness. Unfortunately, the world thinks differently.

If people were to actually follow the guidelines in the Bible, we wouldn't have moral problems in society today. But, it shows that we don't. Just watch the news and take a look at the crime rate. It's pitiful.

To live the life of Jesus as men, we need to have good morals. This would mean practising what the Bible says. Put it into action. Start with the Ten Commandments. Even if you began with the first two (love God and love others), you would be off to a good start. People would see drastic changes in you and be amazed.

Purity
And every man that hath this hope in him purifieth himself, even as he is pure. - I John 3:3

When I think of purity, I think of bottled water. Not only is it a great thirst quencher, it's just so cool to look at. You can see right through it. It's not like a Coke or Kool-aid with it's sugar and added coloring. It's water; pure 'nothing-added' 100% natural water.

Yes, you can get water from rivers and lakes, but I wouldn't advise drinking it. It's muddy and probably has fish cooties in it. Oceans are water, but they're too salty for drinking. Even tap water from your kitchen sink probably isn't pure depending on how your city cleans it. I have read that they add chlorine and aluminum sulfate to it to kill bacteria, but just the sound of having additives mixed in water doesn't sound too cool.

Love
Be ye therefore followers of God, as dear children; and walk in love, as Christ also hath loved us, and hath given himself for us an offering and a sacrifice to God for a sweet smelling savour. - Ephesians 5: 1-2

Jesus loved us enough to lay down his life for us. That's some serious love right there, and if we are to follow His example, we should love others the same. But, for a man in today's world, it's kinda hard.

The world teaches men to not show love or affection when it comes to other men. Its kinda frowned upon and could get your man card revoked. The few slightly affectionate manly responses a man can give another man is a firm handshake, a fist pump and a bear hug - definitely no kissing or butt pats.

Our Hollywood heroes from the movies don't show love or enotions to other men. I hardly believe that a Judo punch to the throat would be considered an affectionate act of love. I don't recall Charles Bronson giving everyone hugs in any of the Death Wish sequels. Can you imagine Clint Eastwood in Dirty Harry saying, "OK fellas. Come on... group hug!" I don't think so.

Even if we don't feel comfortable hugging another man, we can still show love towards them. It can be in our actions by doing good things for them. If you know your neighbor's lawn mower is tore up, offer to cut his yard for free. If he tries to give you money, just refuse it and shake his hand instead. Just be careful and don't express the same feelings you would have for your spouse. That would cause an awkward situation and you could get a Judo punch to the throat.

There will be many opportunities for you to do good things for others. When you are confronted with one, just ask yourself, "What would Jesus do in a situation like this?" And go with it.

Forgiveness
Forbearing one another, and forgiving one another, if any man have a quarrel against any: even as Christ forgave you, so also do ye. - Colossians 3: 13

If we do something that we know is wrong, we get a guilty feeling in our hearts and we simply give it to the Lord. We are all sinners that do stupid stuff and we need forgiveness. We pray to Jesus and ask Him to forgive us. Right? We know that He will because the Bible says He would.

If we are to live our lives that mimics the life of Jesus, we are going to have to learn how to forgive. If someone does us wrong, we are going to have to forgive them. We can't go around holding on to all of this bitterness that we have against them. Let it go.

Compassion
And be ye kind one to another, tenderhearted, forgiving one another, even as God for Christ's sake hath forgiven you. - Ephesians 4: 32

We have to actually care about others like Jesus did when He walked the Earth. This would involve being kind and soft-hearted. These are some of the traits that go against the worldly Man Code. This could be a problem.

If you look around you, you will see that there is always someone in need. There are folks that are down on their luck that need a helping hand. There are people that are disabled or suffer from some type of illness. Compassion is when you realize that these people exist and the world doesn't revolve around you. Compassion is when you take a step to try and help them.

The Bible tells us that Jesus had compassion. He healed the sick, helped the widows and reached out to people in need. If we are looking to Jesus as our role model, then we probably need to be out there helping others, too. It can start with the pan handler that you see on the street that is always asking for money. You know the one. He's the dirty guy that will probably use your money to buy booze or drugs that makes a six-digit money figure from his career as a pan handler. But, then again, he could actually need your help and you refused to help him.

If you know someone that is sick, pay them a visit. It's not that your presence will heal them of their ailment, but it would at least let them know that you care. And that goes a long way.

Endurance
Looking unto Jesus the author and finisher of our faith; who for the joy that was set before him endured the cross, despising the shame, and is set down at the right hand of the throne of God. For consider him that endured such contradiction of sinners against himself, lest ye be wearied and faint in your minds. Ye have not yet resisted unto blood, striving against sin. - Hebrews 12: 2-4

We may never know what it was like to face the things that Jesus did. I personally wouldn't want to. He had to go through a lot of stuff for us. He didn't quit because He knew it was for the greater good.

My definition of 'endure' is the ability to keep going when faced with a challenge. Even though we will never have to face a situation where we will have to die on a cross for the sins of mankind, we will have to endure some things in life. To keep us going in the same direction, we can learn from the life of Jesus.

Some of the things I have endured in life were school, maintaining a job, marriage, raising children and getting older. All of these things have challenges that require some effort on my part. Many times I have had to force myself to keep going, even though I wanted to quit. And believe me, some people actually do.

Can you imagine waking up before the crack of dawn to go to a place to sit in a chair for eight hours to learn about stuff that you know won't help you in the real world? And do it for twelve years? How about going to a place that you really don't care about and work hard to earn money that will eventually be given to someone else? Or how about being in a marriage where there's arguing, nagging and expectations to give of yourself and time to make them happy? Or what about having the reponsibility to train and teach little people to grow up to be oustanding citizens, while at the same time, these trainees rebel against you and the things you try and teach them? Or if you wake up and realize you no longer have the physical ability to do the things you used to do when you were younger? Even though your brain says you can. These are real struggles that we all face in life. What do we do? Quit? Give up? Or endure? Real men following Jesus will endure.

Submission

*Wherefore laying aside all malice, and all guile, and hypocrisies, and envies, and all evil speakings, **as** newborn babes, desire the sincere milk of the word, that ye may grow thereby: if so be ye have tasted that the Lord is gracious. To whom coming, as unto a living stone, disallowed indeed of men, but chosen of God, and precious, - 1 Peter 2: 1-4*

Real men serving God know that they are always a work in progress. There is always something new to learn and there will always be a test in life to show us what we have learned so far.

As men, we are to be submissive to God and His Word to teach us the things we need to know to survive. We know that God is in control of everything. We submit by letting go and letting Him have full control by allowing Him to lead the way. And the great thing is that He knows where He is going.

When we do this, we let go of any selfish pride we may have in ourselves. We become empty vessels for Him to use to do some pretty cool stuff. Submission is basically telling God, "Here... here's my life. Do what You will because I know you know what's best."

Humility and Obedience

*Let this mind be in you, which was also in Christ Jesus: **who,** being in the form of God, thought it not robbery to be equal with God: **but** made himself of no reputation, and took upon him the* *form of a servant, and was made in the likeness of men: and being found in fashion as a man, he humbled himself, and became obedient unto death, even the death of the cross. - Philippians 2: 5-8*

Pride is focused on 'self'. Prideful people believe they deserve better than what life has given them. They become sad, resentful and even jealous of other people and the things they've achieved. From pride comes self-pity, which is a major symptom in depression. People who struggle with pride will live life based on how they feel and expect everyone else to give in to them and flow with their moods.

Two key characteristics of pride are independence and rebellion. We all want our own way about things and we usually will do almost anything to have it our way. This sinful nature leads us to desire independence and we rebel at the thought of being under anyone's control or authority.

People infected by pride typically think so much of themselves that they believe the world should revolve around them. The only thing important to prideful people is getting their needs filled. It may be an emotional need, a desire for attention or a resistance to conform to social norms in order to be seen as an individual. Prideful people struggle with bitterness, revenge, conceit, self-pity, a competitive nature, gossip, slander and vanity. They display a desire to be noticed, which is disguised as shyness. They typically have a lust for attention, approval and praise. Those who attempt to build them up psychologically only assist them in further self-indulgence.

Humility, on the other hand, is a denial of self. It is considering others better than yourself and requires an examination through the Word of God of the actions and attitudes of daily life.

Jesus displayed the ultimate in humility when He came to earth as a human being. He denied Himself and deprived Himself of Heaven and all it's glory for 33 years for us. Because our goal is to become like Jesus in character and attitude, we are to practice how Jesus lived His life. He wasn't concerned about self and put the interest of others before His own.

Being obedient is simply doing what God wants you to do. You will find everything you need to know from the Bible. He puts it all out there for us to follow. We are obedient when we put those words into action.

Kindness
But love ye your enemies, and do good, and lend, hoping for nothing again; and your reward shall be great, and ye shall be the children of the Highest: for he is kind unto the unthankful and to the evil. - Luke 6:35

How do you treat people? I know that's sounds like a strange question. I also know that that it really depends on what 'people' we are referring to because not all people get treated the same.

SON, YOU ARE SO KIND.

THANKS, MOM. IT'S THE LEAST I COULD DO. YOU'VE CHANGED A LOT OF DIAPERS.

POWDERED DONUTS

If the scripture said 'Be kind to your Mom." That would be pretty easy for most of us. We all love our Moms and being kind to her is just the right thing to do. If she can wipe our stinky butts when we were babies, we should be able to say some kind words to her and maybe bring her a flower or two.

If it said, "Be kind to your family and friends", it wouldn't be too hard either. Some of us might have to bite our tongues at the family reunions to keep from saying something mean to Uncle Fred because we know he's as dumb as rocks. We will express our kindness to him when we pass him the biscuits at the dinner table.

But, this scripture refers to three types of people: enemies, the unthankful and the evil. We are supposed to be kind to them because Jesus was. He also tells us to love our enemies. If we are to be men following the words of Jesus, then we should be doing this stuff.

Enemies? These are people that we don't like to socialize with – we avoid them like the plague. If we are in the same room with them, we look the other way. It's for their own protection. A confrontation could get someone body-slammed and it's not going to be me. Right? But, Jesus wants us to love them and love according to Him is an action word. I'm sure it doesn't involve a baseball bat. Maybe a confrontation with an enemy should go like this:

115

(Look your enemy in the eye)

"Do you believe in God?"

THE CONFRONTATION:
LOVE YOUR ENEMY

(Your enemy may clench his fist or he may duck for cover because he is thinking you are about to take him out of this world.)

DO YOU
BELIEVE IN
GOD?

"Do you believe in the Bible and what it says?"

THE
ENEMY

(His fist may loosen up or he may stand at ease because people that talk about the Bible usually just want to talk.)

(OR SIMPLY
SOMEONE THAT
DOESN'T LIKE
YOU)

"Jesus tells me to love my enemies and you are one of them. Do you want to help me do the right thing?"

(Your enemy will now look confused, but he will be open to hear the next thing you have to say.)

"Give me a hug and let's settle our differences."

A scenario like that could have a postive outcome. It could be worth a try. Practice it with your wife at home first after a good argument. You could do some fine tuning until you actually try it on your enemies.

Jesus was kind to the 'unthankful' and the 'evil'. Normal people simply just ignore them. But, here again, we are following Jesus' example and should treat people the way He would.

NOT EVEN A "THANK YOU?
THAT'S IT?!
I AIN'T HELPING
THEM AGAIN!
FORGET IT?!

THE UNTHANKFUL

Those people we have helped in the past that were so ungrateful are considered 'unthankful'. We always said we would never help them again. Well, rethink that thought. Jesus kept on being kind to those people. He didn't write them off like we normally would. He just kept on pouring out kindness from that big old bowl of love. Yes, it will take some practice and patience.

Evil people? Yes, there are folks in this world whose job is to spread meanness and corruption. They wake up in the morning with evil thoughts and desires to disrupt the lives of the innocent. They go to bed at night dreaming of ways to make our lives unbearable. And it's not just our mother-inlaws. There are other evil people in this world, too. But, Jesus wants us to be kind to them.

Maybe being kind is a great way of sharing Jesus with others. I'm sure they don't get to see this trait in other people that they meet. It definitely goes against the way the world would treat them. I read that there are some benefits to us that share kindness to others. I guess they did a scientific study and the results were kind of interesting. It showed that kind people are happier and have better relationships with others. It also says that they have better health and perform better in life. So, maybe being kind has some great rewards for us, too.

Generous giving

Moreover, brethren, we do you to wit of the grace of God bestowed on the churches of Macedonia; how that in a great trial of affliction the abundance of their joy and their deep poverty abounded unto the riches of their liberality. For to their power, I bear record, yea, and beyond their power they were willing of themselves; praying us with much intreaty that we would receive the gift, and take upon us the fellowship of the ministering to the saints. And this they did, not as we hoped, but first gave their own selves to the Lord, and unto us by the will of God. Insomuch that we desired Titus, that as he had begun, so he would also finish in you the same grace also. Therefore, as ye abound in every thing, in faith, and utterance, and knowledge, and in all diligence, and in your love to us, see that ye abound in this grace also. I speak not by commandment, but by occasion of the forwardness of others, and to prove the sincerity of your love. For ye know the grace of our Lord Jesus Christ, that, though he was rich, yet for your sakes he became poor, that ye through his poverty might be rich. - 2 Corinthians 8: 1-9

Giving? That's a tough one. We live in a world that would rather 'take' than give. Here's proof from your local Wally World. The shelves were full of Halloween stuff from September to the last part of October. The next holiday in line is Thanksgiving. This is the holiday where we give thanks. Guess what's on the shelves now starting the first week of November? Christmas stuff! They totally bypassed Thanksgiving. Where's all the cool Thanksgiving ornaments and junk? There may be a small section hidden somewhere, but it's overpowered by all of the Christmas hoopla. It's a shame.

Jesus was a giver. Yes, He could have came down to Earth and built a Man Cave and devoted all of His time doing the things that He wanted to do without the interruption of whiney people trying to consume His time. From the scriptures we know that He was a carpenter's kid. He could have built a woodshop and spent His days building cool things from wood. It could have been anything from tables, countertops to lawn decorations. He had the ability. According to the Bible, Jesus talked a lot about fishing. He could have spent his thirty-three years on Earth doing it. He could have hung out with a bunch of fisherman – whether on the sea or on a creek bank – just living it up talking about fish stuff. They could sit around bragging about their biggest catch or how many lures they have in their tackle boxes. But, He wasn't about all of that. He was a giver.

He gave a lot of His time to strangers that didn't know Him and even to people that really didn't care to know Him. He healed the sick, helped the poor and took the time to teach His followers the things they needed to know after He was gone.

As men followers of Christ, we are to give generously to others, too. It's not always about giving money. I know, personally, that I'm not a fan of giving away something that I have had to sweat and work hard for. I'm sure this has something to do with me growing up in a poor environment as a kid. Thankfully, there are other ways of giving that doesn't involve money.

Time

Time is one of our most valuable assets and shouldn't be wasted. No matter how much money you have, you can't buy more time. Knowing that, we should be using our time more wisely. But, what should we be using our time on? If we look at the life of Jesus, He spent His time interacting with people.

If you look around you in the world today, people are using a lot of their time staring at their cell phones, using their fingers to swipe the screens and doing a lot of thumb action. If you're at a restaurant, dinner isn't about socializing with the people at the table. Everybody has their cell phones in front of their faces. There's not a lot of interaction going on with the people sitting next to them. It seems that technology consumes a lot of people's time.

I remember when my oldest kids were younger. Technology had advanced since my younger days. Computers and gaming systems were more affordable. Every home had one and so did we. My kids used theirs on a daily basis. You would know that they were on them when all you heard was dead silence. There would be days when I didn't even know they were even in the house. They would be cooped up in their rooms playing video games for hours at a time. I think the only time they would come out was to eat or go to the bathroom. I could relate because I was once a kid and knew how cool it was to play video games. Plus, as an adult, I had my own techno-device that kept me occupied as well.

This techno trend went back to the 1980's when I got my first gaming system as a kid. It was the brand new Atari 2600 with the super cool graphics with state of the art color. I would play this thing for hours trying to achieve new levels with hopes of making it to the end. We didn't have cheat codes to help us get further into the game. We would basically get as far as we could go and then cut it off. The rest of the day was spent playing outside with our friends.

As we get older, making money is the goal. The more money you make, the more fun things you can do and the more stuff you can have. But, we learn quickly that making money requires time. In the world today, the meaning of 'time' is considered the same as 'money'. If your goal is achieve financial success, every minute of your day has a dollar value attached. You will see the way you spend your time in terms of monetary gains or financial losses. It's hard to build relationships when 'making money' is your number one priority in life. Unless, of course, youre a salesman and the person you are socializing with is a potential customer.

Jesus was a people-person and used His time interacting with them.

Skills

Everybody has some kind of special ability or skill that they have developed through their lifetime. It could be mental or physical. More than likely, a person is working at a job where they are using that skill and getting paid for it. And that's great!

If that person wants to give like Jesus did, they can offer that skill to someone else in need. Jesus was a carpenter's son. One of the scripture references is Mark 6:3. Families in those days worked together as a unit. I can only assume that Jesus helped His earthly Dad, Joseph, in their family business. If someone needed something fixed, they would call Joseph to come over and fix it. He may have been a handyman and Jesus would have been his hired help or maybe an apprentice. The Bible doesn't get into any details about it, so we have to use our imagination.

A carpenter knows how to build stuff, and if they're repairing something, they are pretty good at figuring out how to put it all back together. If, by chance Joseph was a handyman, he would have had a wide range of skills. Jesus would have learned all of this from him. Knowing the kind of person Jesus was in the Bible, I wonder how many times Jesus helped someone with home repairs or hanging pictures on the wall of an elderly person's home for free. Like I said, the Bible doesn't talk about it, but I have a feeling that He did this quite a bit.

What skills do you have that could help someone in need? I understand that we can't go around working for free every day. We've got bills to pay. That Internet bill isn't going to pay for itself. But, if you know someone in need of your skills, would you be willing to help them? I believe the Lord blesses those that would.

Encouragement

Life can get difficult at times. It seems like the harder we try, the more we fail. That's how it goes. But, then in a month or two, everything turns around and life gets better. We start climbing back up that mountain.

My life has been like a rollercoaster ride in the past ten years. Life was good for a while and then the economy collapsed. Everthing started going downhill. There would be times when it seemed we were going back up and then we would go back down again. When we would reach the bottom, discouragement would set in. We would get depressed and feel like there was no way out of the mess. We would pray to God for help and He would step in at the right time... in His own timing. Through the whole ride, we have learned that God is in control.

One of things I am thanful for are those people He would send our way to offer encouragement when we were at our lowest. They would say the right words to keep us focused on God during the storm. Most of the time they would show up when we were wanting to give up. God uses those bad times to build our faith. It's not that He causes bad things to happen to us because bad things happen to everyone. It's just an opportunity for God to show His strength during our times of weakness. I believe He sends people to keep us encouraged while He works through our lives. These encouragers are vessels that God has chosen to use for His glory in the midst of the storm.

Encouragement is something we all can give to someone. We should allow God to use us to offer the right words to say to someone in need.

Physical Items

If we were to look around our home we would find a bunch of stuff that we no longer use. We would probably find things that we had more than one of – possibly even two or three. If you can no longer park your car in the garage, it's probably because you have it filled with a lot of stuff that you really don't need anyway. If you have considered building a barn or a room addition to your home to store all of the extra stuff you've accumulated, it could be time to evaluate the situation. It could be things you could give to someone else – especially to those that have a need.

I remember years ago visiting my Grandfather in Alabama. He wanted me to help him build a small utility barn on his property. Barns are cool and great for storage, but this is the third one that he has built on this property. One is for his tools, which is great. The second one is for His wife's things, which is kinda cool. The third one? This one would be for his and her extra clothes. They had outgrown the closets inside their home. Keep in mind, my Grandfather came from the Great Depression Era. These people keep everything and don't throw anything of value away.

It seemed to me that the most sensible thing for him to do would be to donate all of them extra clothes to Goodwill or The Salvation Army. He could have just given them to people that needed them. I guess he thought differently and decided to build a barn instead. Maybe those fashions from the 1960's will make a big comeback in the years to come and he will be back in style again. Who knows?

My Stepdad is connoisseur of everything related to cars and fishing. He has been building his inventory of related items for many years. It is something that he enjoys and that's cool.

He has a pole barn dedicated to cars and car related stuff. Even though he doesn't personally work on them due to his disabilities, he has all of the tools, supplies and parts filling the huge square footage of this structure he built many years ago. If you were to walk inside, you would get an overwhelming feeling of claustrophobia. The instant smell of oil, transmission fluid and rubber lets you know that you have stepped into a true Man Cave. The walls are lined with every tool known to man. There are shelves dedicated to parts to cars that he doesn't even own. It's like going to Autozone without all of the fancy signage and good lighting. In addition, his yard contains rare vintage cars that have been long forgotten – neatly lined up along his driveway. This is cool for a car enthusiast and a junk yard employee. If he lived in a subdivision, he would be evicted by the county.

If you ever wanted to know anything about fishing, you would ask this man. He knows everything when it comes to the sport and leisure activity. Even though he doesn't fish much from a pond he had built on his property many years ago, he has enough tools of the trade to make you feel like you just walked into a Bass Pro Shop. He doesn't just have one fishing pole – not even just two or three. He has enough poles to supply the whole state of Georgia and they come in various sizes. Does he have a tackle

box? No, that would be an understatement. He has boxes...
BOXES! And they are all slap full.

But, you have to wonder why people collect so much of
something and yet don't spend time enjoying it themselves. My
Stepdad, with his overabundance of fishing supplies and car-
related items, rarely takes the time to use any of it. Then, I think
of the many years that I have came over for a visit with my kids
when they were younger to
go fishing at his pond. We
would use his fishing stuff.
All we had to do was bring
ourselves. I also think about
the many times when we
needed a tool to repair our
vehicles or needed some
advice on how to fix them.
There have been times
when I had to borrow one
of his cars because ours
would be in the shop. He
would always be there to
help. And it wasn't just us.
His neighbors, his friends
and people he would meet
would receive an open invitation to come over any time for the
same reasons. It was like everything he had was there to share
with someone else. He enjoyed doing it and still does. To me,
that's taking hoarding to a more positive level and that's
awesome.

My wife is a collector of shoes. She would disagree. But, if you have a door hanging shoe rack slap full of flip-flops in various colors, this would make you a collector. Who in their right mind needs flip-flops in all of the colors of the rainbow? I'm not talking about just the basic seven colors – red, orange, yellow, blue, indigo and violet. It's those, plus all of the other hues in between. That makes her a collector – or maybe a borderline shoe hoarder. The interesting thing to me is that our girls wear the same size shoe. They don't mind borrowing them from her whether they ask or not. I haven't asked, but maybe she is stockpiling shoes for them as well. I'll continue to poke fun at her about it, but inside I'll pretend that she is doing it for our daughters.

I guess the point in saying all of this is that we all have extra stuff. No doubt! If we come across someone in need, and we have something that they could use, we could just give it to them from our overstocked inventory. We could free up some space in our overcrowded home and feel good about ourselves when we do.

Infomation
We all know a little bit about something. However, I may not know the things that you know about and vice versa. That's the cool thing about being human beings is that, when we come

together, we can combine our knowledge and become smarter. We can solve some of our problems by sharing our information with each other.

A great example would be in the dreaded car repairs that pop into our lives from time to time. I am not too knowledgeable when it comes to fixing my cars. I can change my oil or replace a tire – mostly the simple stuff. When it comes to something major, I will admit, I need help. That's why I love those awesome people that post the 'How To' videos on YouTube or share car repair information on the Internet. When I get into a pinch and want to save money on car repairs, I will do a little research on the Internet. If a video pops up that is related to what I need to know, I will watch it. If it looks like something I can do myself, I will follow the instructional video and hope for the best. If the video calls for special tools or uses big words, I will know that it's something that only the specialists can handle – not this guy.

There are things that we are good at that could be of some use to someone else. This is the information that we should be willing to give to someone else in need. Maybe we could do our own instructional videos and post them on the Internet. Since blogs are popular, we could write one on topics that we are knowledgeable about and share it on a website. The easiest thing we could do would be to listen to people that we meet. If a need comes up in the conversation, simply fill it.

Despite popular belief, books are still a good source for information. Actually books are easier to obtain than they were several years ago. Yes, many bookstores are now closed, but Goodwill isn't. Ours has two aisles dedicated to this printed information that people are donating every day. If you are like me, you probably have several books that you have read that is now sitting on a shelf collecting dust. You're not going to read them again, so donate them. Share them with someone else.

Some Man Tips From Apostle Paul

Be on your guard; stand firm in the faith; be men of courage; be strong. Do everything in love - 1 Corinthians 16: 13-14

The Apostle Paul was serious about sharing Jesus with the world. It began after he saw the light that changed his life forever on Damascus Road. From there, he used his time writing letters to the churches that he helped start. He would give them tips on how to live life more productively.

Be On Your Guard

Paul knew the importance of living a healthy spiritual life. He knew that there would be things that could easily weed it's way into our life and pull us away from Jesus. His warning "Be on your guard" is simply saying "Be careful! Watch out! Look for the weeds!"

As men living for Christ, this warning is directed to us because we have to protect the things that He has entrusted with us. Our homes, our marriage, our kids and our character as human beings living on Planet Earth are some of those things. We need to stand ready and be able to recognize the things that try to move us from living for Him.

Stand Firm In The Faith

If you are a Christian, you are saying that you are a follower of Jesus Christ. At some point in your life, you have asked Jesus in prayer to forgive you of your sins and to come into your life and save you. From this point, you have decided to live according to what the Bible tells you. You now have faith in Him.

Paul knew that a person could easily lose faith – meaning, to be easily persuaded to follow some other belief or none at all. That's why he warned us to "stand firm in the faith". You may think something like this couldn't happen to you, but it can. Let me ask you, "What would it take for you to turn your back on God and being a Christian all together?"

Unanswered prayers? A death of a close relative? Or how about the feeling you can get when you feel God has made life difficult for you? These are some of the reasons people have given up on their faith.

Life itself with all of its distractions can cause people to lose their faith in Christ. They may know that He exists, it's just that they may no longer have time for Him. They don't go to church, read their Bibles or no longer pray. Paul warns us to stand firm. Standing firm requires us to set priorities in life. As a man living for Jesus, God has to be number one.

Some people just want to live their life how they want to and not have it dictated by God and His 'To Do' list printed in the Bible. They would rather take the reigns of their life and do what they feel would make them happier. It's not going to work. This was a temptation that Jesus faced, too.

And when the tempter came to him, he said, If thou be the Son of God, command that these stones be made bread. But he answered and said, It is written, Man shall not live by bread alone, but by every word that proceedeth out of the mouth of God. - Matthew 4: 3, 4

And then there are those people that will choose their religious faith by which ever one offers the best deal.

"Join our faith and you will receive a free round trip to anywhere you want to go. But wait! There's more! If you act now, we'll throw in this super cool $50 gift card to Wally World... absolutely free!"

LEARN WHY MOST HOLLYWOOD MOVIE STARS ARE JOINING OUR FABULOUS FAITH... VISIT US ON THE WEB.

WWW.SCIENTISTICCOSMETOLOGY.COM

"Join our faith and we will babysit your kids by offering them a bunch of fun things to do. Our state-of-the-art playground will keep them entertained for hours. What's in it for you? Well, for starters, we will stand up here and tell you everything you want to hear. We will make sure you leave here feeling good about yourself – regardless of your current lifestyle and choice of morals. We give warm fuzzies without the guilt."

"Like to eat? We do, too. Join our faith and you'll never have to cook again. We're open twenty four hours a day – seven days a week. When you come,... come hungry!"

What would it take for you to lose faith in God?

Be Men Of Courage
When Paul wrote this to the church in Corinth, he was speaking to people that were Christians living in a time where 'being a Christian' wasn't popular. By living the Christian life, they could have lost their status in society, lost their jobs and economic

opportunities. I imagine they could have lost some friends. It took courage to face the things they faced. It would have been too easy to give up.

What obstacles do we face when we decide to tell the world that we are Christians? I'm sure we will lose some friends. Can you imagine fishing with a friend that you have been fishing with for years? He's been accustomed to talking trash with you and now you've changed. Your new lifestyle change gets his attention. How will he respond? How will you respond? Hopefully all of this Jesus-talk won't get you tossed out of his boat. You may have to learn how to swim. Maybe you should now start wearing a life jacket in case of emergencies.

Be Strong

Being strong is something the world considers more of a physical thing. It considers a man to be one with bulging muscles and washboard abs. But, Paul is referring to spiritual strength. This is something that man can't obtain by himself. He can only rely on God for this type of strength.

I LIFT GRANDBABIES!

IMPRESSIVE.

ARG READER

Finally, my brethren, be strong in the Lord, and in the power of his might. - Ephesians 6: 10

Being a man means knowing that God is that power source for strength. Our job is to make sure we are plugged in. This would involve taking time to study His Word and pray.

Do Everything In Love

Love should be the reason we do the things we do and our purpose for living. We should love God and love everybody else. I'm not saying to go around hugging and kissing on random people. That could get you hurt real fast. Love is more of an action word that requires us to show it in how we treat others.

Beloved, let us love one another: for love is of God; and every one that loveth is born of God, and knoweth God. He that loveth not knoweth not God; for God is love. In this was manifested the love of God toward us, because that God sent his only begotten Son into the world, that we might live through him. Herein is love, not that we loved God, but that he loved us, and sent his Son to be the propitiation for our sins. - 1 John 4: 7-10

It's easy to love our wives, kids and family. Well, it should be anyway. But, loving others may take some practice. A great way to do this is to start looking at people the way that God would. How would He act towards them? When they act stupid or disrespectful towards you, it would be cool to take a moment and see them through the eyes of Jesus. I'm sure He would still see them as stupid and disrespectful, but His actions would be one of mercy, forgiveness and love. Yes, it will take some time to get to this point in life.

Manly Qualifications As Church Leaders

I found some scripture that relate to the type of man that would make a great candidate for church leadership. If these qualifications were considered important for a job in a church, we could use them to better ourselves as men, especially men leading their families and living for Jesus. Here's what I found:

A bishop then must be blameless, the husband of one wife, vigilant, sober, of good behaviour, given to hospitality, apt to teach; Not given to wine, no striker, not greedy of filthy lucre; but patient, not a brawler, not covetous; One that ruleth well his own house, having his children in subjection with all gravity - 1 Timothy 3: 2-4

Likewise must the deacons be grave, not doubletongued, not given to much wine, not greedy of filthy lucre; Holding the mystery of the faith in a pure conscience. - 1 Timothy 3: 8, 9

Blameless

The church in those days needed male leaders with a spotless record. These guys would be respected citizens without a criminal record. They would have needed a good reputation as a person with good morals that always did the right things in life. They were to be blameless because no one could point fingers at them or drag out some gritty news from their past. These were the true 'good fellas'.

Many of the leaders we have in the world today got their high position because they either were friends of someone already in a high position or they were good speakers and knew how to work the crowd. You hear it in the news when media digs up some dirt from their past. This appointed leader has a record of tax evasion, sexual harassment charges or he is not even a born citizen of the country he is being put in charge of. It makes you wonder if good leaders exist anymore. I imagine leaders of today couldn't fit the bill of what the churches from the Bible required.

As men following Jesus, we should live a life that pleases Him. Keep our records clean – do right and act right – in all situations. We should be men of good character. It's important.

Husband Of One Wife

Men from the old days had multiple wives. It was part of their culture before Christianity began. As people were being converted to this new religion, they brought this part of their culture with them. I would assume that the Christian people that were in charge of electing their new leaders felt it wasn't needed. In order to be a leader in the church, they required that this man have only one wife.

What can we apply from this to our life? First of all, polygamy is illegal in the United States. That should be enough reason for someone not to do it, even though people out there are. Secondly, we could apply the possible purposes of why the church didn't want their leader to have more than one wife. The Bible doesn't actually say why so we have to sorta figure it out in our minds.

In the beginning, God created Adam. God didn't want Adam to be alone, so He created for him a woman – not women. He could have created Susie, Samantha, Delores, Jolena, Stephanie and few dozen more, but He didn't. He created one and her name was Eve. I guess God felt that one woman was enough to keep him busy. Adam could have the benefits of having a companion and still have time to manage the other stuff God had entrusted with him.

The same would apply for a church leadership position. If a man is spending all of his time meeting the demands of all of his women, how would he have time for the church? He wouldn't. Let's look at our own lives for a moment. How much time do we spend doing the things our wives want us to do – you know, the Honey-Do lists? Now multiply that time by the number of wives that these old guys had. They probably didn't have any time left.

Having multiple wives probably isn't a problem with men these days. Some men seem to put other men on a higher pedestal based on how many girlfriends they currently have, women they've slept with or how many 'baby mamas' they have in their line up. The more you have, the higher the rank.

Maybe being a man in God's eyes is the one that chooses to stick with one. This shows true devotion and a willingness to work out relationship problems. You will know this guy isn't a quiter.

Vigilant

A vigilant leader in those days were men that had the ability to keep a close watch over the church. They could recognize potential problems before they turned into something major. Because the word is mentioned before 'sober' tells me that this person had to have a clear mind and the ability to think.

Life is busy in present day. There is so much going on around us with so many distractions. It's easy for us to lose focus on the things that are the most important — God, our wives, our kids and relationships with others.

As men, we should strive to put things into perspective by priortizing things in our life. We could learn to turn our brains off to the things that really don't matter and turn them on to the more important ones. This is where we should really focus.

Sober

Yes, drinking went on in the old days. People would get drunk. Being drunk is the opposite of being sober. A man applying for a leader position at a church had to be sober. I'm sure this position required a leader to be focused and we all know what drinking too much can do to our mental stability.

Even though it is cool to hang out with our buddies watching football and drinking beer, I think we need to know our limits. There will be many times where we will have to make decisions that could affect our families and people around us. We should keep a level head at all times and not be a drunkard. Drunks don't have the reputation of making good decisions. If they did, they wouldn't be walking the streets peeing in public places. They wouldn't be listed in the local arrest log for DUI.

As men serving the Lord, we don't want this kind of reputation.

Of Good Behavior

Having good behavior means that you realize that you are not the only one that fills the space in the small area of the world that you are standing. You will realize that how you act will affect those around you. So, your behavior will be considerate of those people.

If you are acting in a way that causes people to frown and point fingers at you, chances are you are showing signs of bad behavior. If cops are called and put you in handcuffs, this could be side effects of your bad behavior. If you are currently in jail serving time,... yes, it was caused from your bad behavior. The church from the Bible did not want this kind of man as a leader. I can see why.

As men serving the Lord, we should be men of good behavior. We should act right and do things that create a peaceful atmosphere to those around us. People shouldn't be calling the cops on us. It wouldn't be a good thing.

Given To Hospitality

My wife is probably the most hospitable person I know. She will open the doors of our home to anyone. She will feed them and put clothes on their back if they need them. I, on the other hand, am not so giving. It's probably because I have seen the people that she has been hospitable to. They tend to stay around my home way too long. They wear out their welcome real quick.

Our house is small but it's big enough for the four of us. If a person were to spend the night, the only spot available for them would be on the couch. We don't have extra bedrooms or additional bathrooms to accommodate a weary traveler passing by – and definitely not their entire family.

Several years ago, my wife and I were going through a financial situation because the economy was in a mess. We, like many other Americans, struggled to make ends meet. A friend of ours was struggling finacially and was about to lose his home. He lost his job and had no where to go. My wife, being the soft-hearted person she is, offered to help. She miraculously made some space in our living room for him to stay while he got his life together. Days turned into weeks. Weeks turned into months. Finally, he got a job, a place to live and he moved. I was relieved.

Also, a few years ago, my wife offered our home to a family of six. This family's home burned down from an accidental fire. They had no place to live, no clothes and no food. My wife stepped up to the plate and helped them. These people slept in my living room. They finally found a new place to live a few months later and moved. I was overjoyed.

MAXIMUM LIVING ROOM CAPACITY

4 PEOPLE
(AND THAT'S IT)

WIFE

When my older kids were teenagers, they had friends that would spend the night with us. Many of them were having family problems. My wife felt it neccessary to turn our small home into a Troubled Teen Hotel. She said it would keep them off the streets and away from possible danger. That may have been true, but why sacrifice our limited food supply and share our Internet to bunch of punks that like to eat while sitting on my couch thumb wrestling on their cell phones all day. I'm glad they're all grown and out of my house.

I'm cool with the whole 'being hospitable' thing as long as it can be done far away from my safe zone. My home is where I come to relax. It is where I find peace and can communicate with the ones I care about most – my family. It is very hard for me to do this with a house full of strangers. Not only do I have to provide shelter for them, but I have to give them food and hours of entertainment. All I want to do is relax.

I'm sure my wife is doing everything the Biblical way. She has a good heart and people love her. She does a lot for the community and I'm sure she has changed the lives of many people. I will continue to support her endeavors, while keeping my feelings about it to myself. Maybe one day I will be as hospitable as she is, but I seriously doubt it.

The church from the Bible wanted a leader that would be willing to open its doors to those in need and basically place a welcome mat at its entrance doors. As men living for Jesus, we should be just as welcoming to others, especially to the people we can help.

Apt To Teach
The church wanted their candidate for leadership to be able to teach. This would involve having knowledge about the subject

they would be teaching and hopefully would have good people skills. But, most importantly, this man would need to have the desire to want to teach them.

In today's world, a teacher is a job position that comes with a paycheck. Unless, of course, if it's in the church. It's usually filled by volunteers. But, people don't realize that almost everyone has an opportunity to teach someone something. Even as old as I am, I am still learning new stuff and someone is teaching it to me.

Technology is a good example of this because it is constantly changing. If you don't stay on top the latest gadgets and gizmos, you'll be left in the dark. Kids these days make the perfect teachers for showing us older folks how these things work. I personally do not like cell phones. They're too small and I can't stand talking on one. People only call you when you're driving, working or using the bathroom. It's hard to do any of these things when you're on a cell phone and I'm not going to wear a headset because they just look weird. But, I hear they are great for doing web searches on the go and typing back and forth to your friends, which is called texting. I can do these things fairly well, and if I come across something I don't know how to do yet, I can always ask my eight year old daughter. She is very helpful.

When computers first came out, I was on top of the scene. I took the time to learn as much as I could about them. I knew that one day computers would be very popular and everyone would have one. As they evolved, I tried to follow along and keep up with the lastest changes and upgrades. The negative side to this is when you get constant phone calls from your mother-inlaw wanting you to help her with her personal computer. You end up wasting hours of your day to finally learn that she has deleted important system files that are now in her recycle bin on her desktop. Then you have to explain over and over of why you shouldn't delete stuff. Just because you can't pronounce the file name doesn't mean it's not important.

I believe everyone has something that they are knowledgeable about and should be willing to share that knowledge with someone else. Living life, in general, has taught us so much through experiences - good and bad. We could take what we have learned and teach it to our children and the younger generation. It could save them from making the same mistakes or wasting away years of trying to learn something on their own. That's why kids should listen to the older generation and respect them. These wrinkly people have some priceless insight on life that could be very beneficial to their well-being. They need to listen.

The younger generation also has some information that us old folks should be willing to listen to and learn from. We can't go through life thinking "you can't teach an old dog new tricks" and feel like we know it all. Not only can they keep us on top of the latest computer gadgets, these kids can keep us fashionably in-style and current with the latest trends. Who knows? You may learn that the polyester you have in your closet is actually an ancient fabric from the past – worn exclusively by cavemen. Wouldn't that be something?

POLYESTER.

As men serving the Lord, we have to realize that we are here to teach others. Those skills and life lessons that we have learned can also be used to teach another generation.

Not Given To (Much) Wine
This topic is very similar to the one about being sober. But, because of the wording, 'not given', it almost sounds like it is referring to a person with a drinking problem. It could be talking about an alcoholic.

ONE FOR NOW ...
AND ONE FOR THE ROAD.

Alcoholism is a disease. However, it can be cured. A man seeking a leadership role with the church back in those days shouldn't have an addiction to alcohol. This would be worse than the occasional drink. It would mean that he wouldn't be able to function without it.

Here again, as men, we need to be able to think clearly. We shouldn't be controlled by alcohol. If it has become a problem, we should seek help and get our lives back on track.

No Striker

I had to do some research on what a striker is because it is a word that we don't normally use. It is not a term used in baseball either. A striker is a person that is quick to scold others especially when they aren't doing what they are supposed to do. They usually make people feel less than human when they do this. A man that

NERD
WORMY
WIMP
GEEK
DORK
LOSER

149

does this would not get a leadership position in a church from the Bible.

You've heard the saying, "Sticks and stones may break my bones, but words will never hurt me." That's a load of crap. Words do hurt and can create scars that last a lifetime. A perfect example would be our memories from elementary school. Do you still remember some of the negative names kids may have called you from way back then? For some of us, it's really no big deal now, but back then those words hurt and changed our life.

As men for Christ, we have to choose our words wisely when we are dealing with people. We should use our words to build others up instead of tearing them down. We have to watch what we say to our wives and children, especially when we are arguing with them. Because whatever we say, they will remember.

Not Greedy Of Filthy Lucre
Greed is a selfish desire for something. It usually refers to things such as money and power. People that are considered greedy will do just about anything to get those things they want with no regards to the people they hurt to get it.

If you had a pie sitting on a table with eight people ready to eat it, the greedy one would want to eat the whole thing by themselves. They could care less if the other seven got to eat any at all. Even though splitting the pie into eight evenly slices would be the right thing to do, the greedy person would figure out how to get the whole pie. He couldn't be happy and content with his one slice.

Unfortunately, the world works the same way. Take a close look at the banking industry, insurance companies, the medical field and so many others. You can definitely see it in big businesses when they compete for a bigger slice of the pie. Growing a company is cool if its purpose is to serve others and offer more jobs to people that need them. If money and getting rich is it's only purpose, it's priorities are wrong.

On a smaller scale, if we focus more time in our day trying to obtain wealth, then we will neglect everything else – including the things in life that are more important.

The church from the Bible wanted a leader that was not greedy because they knew that he would be more focused on accumulating stuff and not on God and the church. The Bible teaches about contentment and God's provision. As men serving the Lord, we should be more focused on Him. He will provide for our needs. That's a promise from His Word. He is in charge of your life. If He wants you to have more, He will provide it.

Be Patient
Having patience is one of those things that we simply don't have 'patience' for. Nobody likes to wait. We live in a fast-paced world

with so much to do and a short time to get it done. We want express lanes to everything we want out of life.

In the old days when a family wanted to go out and eat, you took the time to drive to the restaurant, order the food and wait for the waitress to bring it to you. While you waited, the family could actually talk with one another. When the food finally arrived, it would be hot and worth the wait. Everyone would leave satisfied and the table conversation strengthened the family as a group.

These days, eating at a restaurant is more about filling that empty gap in our stomachs. It has to be delivered quickly. It's no longer about a quiet evening of family bonding. If you were to look at the tables in a restaurant around you, you would see that every family member has a cell phone in their face. No one is talking. They're communicating, but not with each other.

A lot of families don't have time for the whole dine-in experience. They would rather use the restaurant's drive-thru option because you can quickly order your food and pick it up at the next window. You can then eat it on the go in the privacy of your own car as you hurriedly drive to your next appointment.

THE WORKPLACE

HOME

EARLY... AGAIN.

ARG READERS

Everybody has to work and some of us have to drive to get there. It would be great if everyone could work from home or lived next door to the company that pays our salary. But, that's not how life works. The expressway is a great way of travel that gets us to our working destination. These roads are much different than your casual Sunday drive where you take the time to look at the scenery. It's like a Nascar race with a bunch of crazy drivers changing lanes unexpectedly and making bad driving decisions all in an effort to report to their place of employment. You have to be alert and in 'defense mode' at all times. Chances are, someone will be involved in a wreck today. Your only hope is that it's not you. On the expressway, the minimum speed is usually around 70 MPH, and if you're among the drivers that accidentally slept late that morning, it will be much faster. There's no time for sight-seeing or the casual joy ride. It's a

SPECIAL DELIVERY.

I JUST ORDERED IT.

UPS

MORE STUFF, INC

stressful, rage-filled race to get a paycheck and it happens every day.

People are in a hurry and want things now. They want instant gratification for everything in life. Technology has made it easy for people that don't like waiting in long lines because you can now do what you want in the privacy of your own home. You can make reservations online for restaurants. You can stream movies instantly. And you no longer have to join the massive crowd of crazy shoppers at your local Wally World. You can order anything you want online and have it delivered to your house – many times in just 2 days. That's unbelievable. But, that's how it's become in society. Who needs patience when you no longer have to wait?

One of the things that technology hasn't truly improved is in our relationships with others. Yes, it has helped us to reach long lost friends that we haven't seen in a very long time. Yes, it has helped us to communicate with people through the use of emails, texting and video chatting. But, what about the 'one-on-one in-your-face' type of communication that you do when you are in the same room with someone? That's not too common anymore. It's inconvenient and it soaks up too much time. Plus, people can be annoying and can get on our nerves. It's hard to escape them. Technology makes it easier by allowing us to shut off a conversation with a press of a button or the option of not replying. If we're honest with ourselves, we simply don't have patience with people. It could be because they don't match up to the expectations we have of them.

The church from the Bible wanted a patient leader. It's probably because this person could handle stressful situations. Instead of wanting things to go their way in their time frame, this person would have the ability to wait and not make sudden decisions that could affect the outcome in a negative way. They would also be able to work well with others.

As Christ-minded men, we should develop more patience. Studies show that people with patience enjoy better mental health because they are able to handle stress better. Less stress means we can live healthier and possibly live longer. It can make us better people and help us to achieve our goals because we're not making drastic decisions or avoiding obstacles in life.

Not A Brawler

A brawler is someone that likes to fight. The solution to many problems in life can be solved with a fist punch to the face according to the mind of a brawler. If there aren't any problems to solve, they create them by starting unneccessary fights for pure fun and personal enjoyment. I have always tried to avoid these people.

I remember many years ago being a child in school and riding a school bus. These young brawlers could always be found sitting in the last few seats in the back. You couldn't talk with them or even look them in the eye. I guess they would feel intimidated and would try to start a fight with you. If you did the right thing and walked away, it would only make matters worse. You had two choices – either fight them or be labeled by everyone as a chicken. If I knew I had the chance of winning, I would take them up on their offer. If it was a guarantee that I would lose the fight, I would back away, grow my feathers and start clucking like any smart young person would do.

Now that I look back, some of these kids were trying to display their 'manliness' by being rough and tough. It could have been because of how they were raised. That's understandable. But, some of the others could have had a psychological disorder and needed medication. They could have had insecurity issues or suffered some kind of abuse, but we don't think about this sort of stuff when we are kids. It's kind of interesting how many of these kids got older and either served time in jail or are currently serving time. And some of them got their act together before they ended up there.

As an older man, I don't see fighting as a way to show my 'alpha male' to anyone. It's probably because men my age either don't care or we have been married with children so long that life has pretty much knocked us down a few notches. We have learned to survive by just keeping the peace.

Fighting isn't always about throwing punches. There are people out there who feel their job in life is to stir up trouble and cause arguments. You see this a lot on social media. We call these people trolls or drama queens. It seems they are always against anything you post on your social media page. They will leave negative comments, purposely argue with you and sometimes act childish with name calling. To me, this is a type of brawler.

The church from the Bible did not want this kind of man as a leader. They would be troublemakers and would cause problems in the church. For men serving Christ today, it just doesn't reflect Jesus in our lifestyle. He wasn't about all of this.

Not Covetous
Covetous people have a great desire for wealth and the possessions of others. The church mentioned in the Bible did not want this kind of man in charge of their church. It's kind of funny because the church leaders that come to mind from TV seem to

fit in this category. They are the ones with the paid actor that speaks the sales pitch at the end of their sermons.

"If you liked today's sermon, you can order it now for the low low price of just $19.95 plus shipping and handling. But wait! There's more! If you act now, we'll throw in this sweaty towel he used to wipe his face with for free!"

Or how about the preacher that walks on stage with a shovel telling the audience that if you donate a shovel of money to his church, God will reward them with a whole lot more. I'm sure the ones that did were greatly disappointed, but at least the preacher got something out of it. Things like multiple mansions with luxury cars could create a lavishing lifestyle for someone that loves material wealth. I'm just glad that many of these covetous preachers were arrested for their crimes.

What could be the problem for a church whose leader desires great wealth? I guess the real question is what does a church leader have to do to obtain great wealth to fufill his desire? Lie? Cheat? Make people feel comfortable in their sin so that they will show up for his sermons and freely give him money? He would have to reword the scriptures and preach a false doctrine that people would enjoy. That wouldn't be a good thing.

Asking for money to help support your church or ministry isn't a bad thing. It's a neccessity. However, if the purpose of your church or ministry is to create great wealth and a luxurious lifestyle for its leaders, then you have a problem.

Men, that have chosen to serve the Lord and to allow Him to mold them to be like Him, would have a hard time being covetous. He would be a reflection of Jesus and covetness would go against His character. Jesus didn't lie, cheat, deceive or kill people. He had a mission of love and we should, too.

One That Ruleth Well His Own House
The Bible plainly says that men should be the leaders of their home. If they can't lead their home, they definitely wouldn't make a good candidate for leadership of a church. I guess the people in charge of selecting the rightful candidate would first check out his family. If his kids were rebelliously out of control and his wife had him hen-pecked, he would automatically be disqualified.

What does it mean for a man to rule his house? When we think of the word 'rule', we may think of a ruler of a country. Rule is a negative word because of the way these leaders choose to rule over their subjects. Creating strict laws and regulations with strong penalties for not following them, waging war to conquer territories and increasing taxes becomes part of the characteristics of a ruler. Even though we elected this ruler over us and expected him to be a leader that has our best interest in mind, he is visualized as a narcissitic sociopath. Sadly this term could be used to describe men that 'rule' over their home.

The Bible gives us more information on how men are to lead and rule his own house. Because there is so much to say, we will talk more about it in the next few pages.

Be Grave
Likewise must the deacons be grave, not doubletongued, not given to much wine, not greedy of filthy lucre; Holding the mystery of the faith in a pure conscience. – 1 Timothy 3: 8, 9

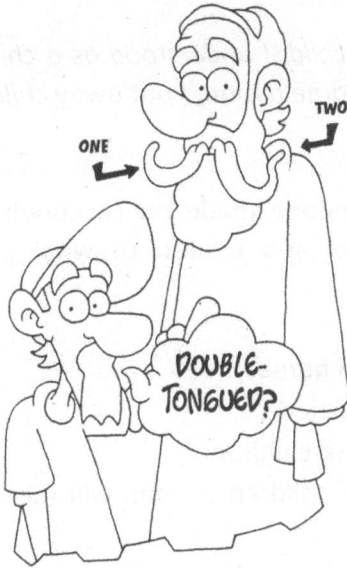

ONE

TWO

DOUBLE-TONGUED?

Grave? I included the verse for this because this word has quite a few meanings according to Webster. The one I think that relates the most is 'to be serious and solemn' which is characterized by sincerity. The church from the Bible wanted a leader that would be serious and devoted to their duties. They didn't want someone that was 'doubletongued', which I think means to live a double life. An example would be a person that acts holy on church day and then like a heathen throughout the week. They didn't want a leader like this. From these verses, Paul is simply saying that the man who would lead this church should be a believer who is mature, who knows the basic elements of the gospel and whose life matches his profession of faith.

This could apply to us, as men professing to be Christian leaders of our home. We could go to church and do all of the Jesus-stuff around people outside of the four walls of our house. We would look good to them. But, how do we act around our family? Do they see Christ in us? Our kids look up to us and will probably become like us when they are older.

Or vice versa. We could be the good Christian example at home, but how do we act when we are around people outside of our home? We need to act the same bothways.

Be A Man – Not A Child

When I was a child, I spake as a child, I understood as a child, I thought as a child: but when I became a man, I put away childish things. - 1 Corinthians 13: 11

I borrowed this from a post someone made on Facebook the other day. I thought it was cool and related to what I am studying. Here's what it said:

- Boys play house. Men build homes.
- Boys shack up. Men get married.
- Boys make babies. Men raise children.
- A boy won't raise his own children. A man will raise his and someone else's.
- Boys invent excuses for failure. Men produce strategies for success.
- Boys look for somebody to take care of them. Men look for someone to take care of.
- Boys seek popularity. Men earn respect by knowing how to give it.
- Boys quit and walk away when things get hard. Men will promise to love you through it all.
- Refuse to be a little boy. Be a man.

Before I started writing this book, I gathered all of my information that I wanted to share. I also asked my younger kids what I thought was an important question.

"Can you name 5 people that you know that you consider to be a man?"

I thought it was a pretty simple question, but both of them looked at me a little confused. They thought a bit more about it and finally gave me five people as examples. Jesus made their list, which I thought was cool. They named a few celebrity figures and even included their Grandfather. That was nice. The sad thing to me was that I didn't make their list of people, so I asked them why.

DAD, YOU'RE NOT A MAN. YOU'RE A KID!!

They laughed at me and said, "Dad, you're not a man. You're a kid."

Their comment blew me away. I was in shock. I had to rethink my whole life story and make sure that their statement wasn't true. I feel like I have always met the description of a man. I have been a good husband and father. I even stepped up to the plate to be a father to kids that I didn;t give birth to. I work every day. I mange our home. In my heart, I know I am a man. Well, with one exception. I like to have fun with my kids. I enjoy laughing and playing with them. I'm a cartoonist by nature and my personality seems to match. My brain is full of humor and I tend to find a joke in most of life's situations. I can be serious at times, but it usually doesn't last long. I even play practical jokes on my wife whether she wants me to or not. Some folks may consider this as acting childish, but I consider it as part of who I am. Does this disqualify me as a man? Is being a man totally the opposite? I would hope not.

The scripture in 1 Corinthians calls out three things about a child that should change as we become men:

I spake (spoke) as a child
I understood as a child
I thought as a child

Speaking Like Children

When a child is born, they don't speak. For the most part, they makes noises and usually cry when they want something. It's mostly for things like food and a quick diaper change. If they are sick or uncomfortable in their surroundings, they will let you know by making a loud shrieking noise that also turns into tears. As parents, we usually have to experiment with a few comforting things until their crying stops. Mothers are generally better at this because they were created with the food source attached to their chest. Plus, the fact that they carried this child in their womb for nine months and have a better understanding of what this child wants. Dads have to go with the flow and learn. Or they can do like I did and pass the child on to it's mother after he has tried everything possible.

Thankfully babies grow older and learn to speak. It begins with small words, but they are able to give us a general idea of what they want. My granddaughter is two and says, "Ba-ba." We have learned through experience that she is telling us that she wants her sippy cup. In a few short years, I am sure she will be able to say, "Dearest Grandfather, could you please deliver the tall glass of iced tea from the countertop in the kitchen? I would most appreciate this kind act of brave grandparenting. I would get it myself, but unfortunately I am vertically-challenged and my mother doesn't want me climbing ladders." But, she hasn't gotten to this point yet.

DEAREST GRANDFATHER?!! I'M PARCHED.

Other than casual conversation, it seems like a child mostly speaks to us when they want something. This goes on throughout their childhood years and even after they are grown and married. It feels good knowing that my kids need me for something. However, I have to stop myself from jumping to every need. Kids need to learn to do things on their own and develop the basic skills of survival.

Being a man would mean not calling Mom or Dad for everything, especially if you're in your thirties with a full grown beard and moustache. That's just not cool. Also, whining and crying when things don't go your way or everytime you need something wouldn't be too manly around your friends and co-workers. If you do this around a woman, her natural instinct could kick in and she might just warm you up a bottle or bring you a pacifier.

Understanding And Thinking Like Children

For the most part, kids are self-centered. Many of them feel like the world revolves around them. As parents to these cute little creatures that we created, we're cool with that and we try to cater to their every need. That's why we jump through financial hoops for their birthdays and at Christmas time.

What would you like for your birthday this year, Susie-dear?

Charlie-pumpkin, what do you hope Santa brings you for Christmas?

We try to meet their expectations. But, it's not always the kids fault. I think, as parents, we also try to give our kids more than what we had when we were kids. Because of that, we are adding fuel to the fire by creating little 'all about me' humans that will carry this mindset into their adulthood life. They become accustomed to getting 'what they want' and 'when they want it'.

As grownups, if they don't change, they will pout like little babies when they don't get that job promotion or steak for dinner that they feel they deserve. They will get easily discouraged and give up when things don't happen the way they expected them to.

Maybe my girls don't fully understand what being a man means. I don't speak, understand or think like a child. Maybe the world is teaching them that real men don't show emotions created from fun and laughter. Maybe they are being taught that men should be rough and tough and not playful or worse... not involved with their children at all. I don't plan on changing my ways any time soon. I hope I can teach them what the Bible says about what real men should be and the things they need to know to become adults that serve the Lord. Time will tell.

Ten Essential Characteristics Kids Need To Learn Now

Then were there brought unto him little children, that he should put his hands on them, and pray: and the disciples rebuked them. But Jesus said, Suffer little children, and forbid them not, to come unto me: for of such is the kingdom of heaven. And he laid his hands on them, and departed thence. - Matthew 19: 13-15

And Jesus called a little child unto him, and set him in the midst of them, And said, Verily I say unto you, Except ye be converted, and become as little children, ye shall not enter into the kingdom of heaven. Whosoever therefore shall humble himself as this little child, the same is greatest in the kingdom of heaven. - Matthew 18: 2-4

From the scriptures, Jesus loved children. Actually, He encouraged us to come to Him as children. What is it about them that caught His interest? According to research that I discovered on the Internet, there are ten essential characteristics that kids need to learn in their early years and continue to develop into their adult life. Unfortunately, life these days has become too busy or too distracting that some kids won't get to learn them. Here's what I found:

Curiousity
A child should be curious about their environment. It's normal. There's so much to see, hear, smell, taste and touch. They're new to everything and should ask questions about it – lots of questions. Parents are the ones that should be answering all of those questions for them.

Mom, why is the sky blue?

How come leaves are green in the Spring and turn red in the Fall?

What is this brown thing on the ground? It fell out of Fido's butt when he lifted his tail up.

It's questions like this that need answers. Unfortunately, many of us are too busy and find it easier to just ignore them. Eventually, the child will quit asking questions because they are now no longer interested in the world around them. They will think that their constant questions are burdens to their parents. They will be content to learn just the basics for their survival and ignore everything else.

This will continue into adulthood. Grown people just don't care anymore. They don't want to learn anything else. The world around them has become dull. I think we need to get excited about life again and learn as much as we can about everything. Stimulate the brain and ask questions. Use the Internet to do research and learn more. The more you know, the more you grow.

Social Skills
I have seen a change in the way we socialize and interact with people in my lifetime. The simple thing as playing games has went from an activity that was done outside with other kids to

being able to do it in the privacy of your own home with a computer and a Wi-Fi connection. There's not a whole lot of one-on-one interaction.

It's been said that kids with good social skills tend to do better in school, have a better self-image and are better at resolving conflicts. I believe this, because when I was a kid in school, it seemed that the popular kids made the good grades and excelled in just about everything. They were given better opportunities that later resulted in better jobs with more income as an adult. I think it all centered around good social skills that their parents taught them at a young age.

As parents, we need to let our kids play with others at the local playground. Get them involved in activities with other kids by signing them up for Karate lessons and baseball. The first step would be to cut them video games off and make them little Hobbits go outside and play. Go next door and tell your neighbors to do the same. It will seem a little awkward at first, but let them know you are trying to save the human race. They'll understand.

It's not too late for the older folks. We got to get off those computers and maybe take a trip to Wally World or wherever tons of people gather together. We could start by making random conversations with the buggy pushers. Talk about anything as long as we interact with people. Maybe we could use our cell phones for actually talking to people instead of snooping on them on social media. Instead of posting status updates every five minutes, we could learn to tell people what we're doing in person with that hole in our face that God gave us. We could communicate using our own natural facial expressions instead of those goofy emoji things that are popular today.

We have to make 'being social' a priority in life and make it personal. Step out from behind those computer screens and meet someone face to face.

I'M OK!... SOMETIMES 'LIFE' HAS A WAY OF TRIPPING YOU UP AND KNOCKING YOU DOWN. I'LL GET MYSELF TOGETHER AND GET BACK UP IN A MINUTE.

LIFE

Resilience

To have resilience is having the abiltity to get up and stand after life has knocked us down. We are all going to face problems in life that will make us choose between trying to solve it or walking away from it. It would be great if we had developed good problem solving skills at a younger age because a lot of problems can be solved. Also, many problems aren't as big when we take the time to analyze it and put it into perspective.

As parents, we don't want our sweet precious angels to go through any kind of problem. We want them to live their youth floating down an everflowing stream of creamy milk chocolate with sugar sprinkles. We take the Vanilla Ice approach when it comes to our kids, "If there's a problem,... Yo! I'll solve it!" The sad thing is that the child won't develop the skills needed to handle problems in life when they get older. It could be why they are still living in your basement at thirty years old.

We should teach our kids how to solve problems. When they face an obstacle, step back and let them deal with it. If they need our help, they will ask. But, don't be so quick to come to the rescue. Give them a chance to handle it themselves first. Maybe instead of solving it for them, we could just work with them and solve it together.

If you're thirty years old and living in your parents basement, the time is now to get on your feet and move on. You will face problems in life and will have to deal with it. Thank those loving parents for allowing you to live in their home this long and for the free unlimited use of their electricity and Wi-Fi. Get a job if you don't already have one. Save a few paychecks and find a new place to live. Pack your bags and move on. Resilience begins now. You will do fine.

Integrity
You've heard the saying, "If you don't stand for something, you'll fall for anything." This speaks of having values in life; a certain

code of conduct that we should live by. There should be things we know we shouldn't do or ways we shouldn't act. This is all part of our values that should have been instilled in us from the day we were born by our parents. Having integrity means we live by those codes and values. For those of us that live according to what the Bible says, our values come from what it teaches us. This is just a tip of the iceberg:

Love
Courteous
Patience
Forgiveness
Compassion
Respect
And so much more

For example, if you valued love, your personality and the way you treated others would reflect it. You would be kind and look out for their best interest. If you valued being courteous, your automatic response in public places would be to open doors for others and phrases like 'thank you' and 'yes, please' would be a common thing to say.

Parents should be teaching these good values to their child at a young age. This would involve disciplining them when they do wrong and rewarding them when they do right. But, most importantly, we need to make sure that we are leading by example by showing good values ourselves. Kids learn visually and will learn by what they see in you. If you're not going teach it, they will learn from other sources that may not be good for them.

Being courteous to others is one of the things I value. I open doors for others and it's not because I'm trying to be a gentleman and only open them for the women. I open doors for men, too. Yes, sometimes I get weird looks, but I am hoping it shows my respect for others. It has become a habit and even awkward at times. I can have my hands full of grocery bags, but I will do my best to open doors for people with my leg. I have become a contortionist in this area of being courteous. My kids do it, too. It makes me proud to see my son carry on this personal value. However, teaching my daughters when its appropiate to do it is a little challenging. Men open doors for women and not the other way around, unless they are grandfathers with one qualifying grandchild. We're still working on this.

As men, we need to learn and practise good values. Stay true to what we believe and be men of integrity.

Resourcefulness
Being able to find solutions to your problems is defined as resourcefulness. Living the easy life in a home where you have parents that take care of your every need could hinder learning this basic survival trait. Here's an example:

UMM... MOM? DAD? I GOT A MAJOR PROBLEM.

A MINOR CRISIS THAT LOOKS MAJOR

If your answer to every problem you face in life is, "Call Mommy or Daddy.", then you might have a real crisis and it's not the original problem. It's your sole dependency upon your parents. You have got to learn to let go of those apron strings.

My youngest daughter is cool. She is very smart and watches educational videos on YouTube on her tablet. She likes the videos called Life Hacks or 5 Minute Crafts because it teaches her how to use normal everyday items to solve problems. For example, if you wanted to heat up a dinner roll you had the night before, without it being hard as a brick, you would pour water on top of it first before sticking it into the microwave. It's simple and easy and it solved a problem. For an eight year old to know how to do this, I think it's awesome. To be able to make a small outside grill for cooking food from a couple of tin cans, wood and a match lets me know that this girl would do fine if she had to survive out on her own. To make a cell phone stand up on a table surface with the simple use of a zip tie means that one day this girl will be able to handle many more life problems she will face in the future. This makes me proud. She's going to be OK.

My older kids are learning how to survive and deal with everyday problems. They don't fall apart at the seams as much as they did in the beginning. Being out on their own without parental interference has taught them to rely on themselves and their spouses for solutions. Every now and then we will get an occasional phone call asking for advice on how to deal with something and that's OK. We're all at an age where advice is more acceptable than handling their problems for them. I am thankful that my kids look to me for advice, but I am also thankful that they have tried to solve their problems themselves first.

Creativity

I am an artist. I enjoy drawing, writing and playing music. I have always tried to allow my kids to express themselves artistically. I strongly encouraged it. The day my son showed an interest in music by banging cooking utensils on our pot and pans, I went out and bought him a drum set. He's been playing ever since. When my oldest daughter showed an interest in writing poetry, I encouraged her by sharing mine with her with hopes to inspire her to keep going. When my middle daughter would listen to music and dance all over my living room, I immediately signed her up for dance classes. When my youngest daughter showed an interest in reading at three years old, I began buying her books. Creativity opens a door to a big world of imagination and helps define ourselves. It helps us with our communication and problem solving skills and emotional development.

When companies are looking for people to hire, they generally look for creative people. Why? Because creative people think outside of the box and find solutions to problems. They are enthusiastic to try new things and aren't afraid to fail. They are usually energetic and always thinking of ways to make improvements. The alternative would be someone that lacks the fire to work and is only there for a paycheck.

Being creative is something we all could benefit from.

Empathy

We should all care for others and should have been taught this at an young age. If we see someone in need, our first response should be to help. It seems the world is morally declining and people just don't care about others anymore.

A homeless man on the side of the road holding a sign asking for food to eat should be an opportunity for us to show empathy. But, it doesn't. For most of us, we look away and hope he doesn't catch a glimpse of our eyes. We don't want the confrontation. I mean, he's probably not really even homeless. He'll probably buy drugs with it and noone wants to further a man's drug addiction problem. Plus, we heard on the news that scam artists are now disguising themselves as homeless people with signs, especially at Christmas time. Who's to say that this guy isn't one of them? Drive on.

We've all heard about the starving kids in Africa. It's sad and we would like to help, but there's something fishy about the paid actress spokesperson that sadly pulls at our heart strings on the commercials about it. The rumor is that a large percent of the donated food funds goes directly into her own personal refrigerator. She looks healthy enough so the rumor could be true. Turn the channel.

And then there's those family members with illnesses or in the hospital. Unfortunately, our life is so busy that we can't offer any help. I mean, we do care about them. If we didn't, we wouldn't post sweet words on their Facebook wall like, "Praying for you!" or "Hope you get better soon! Keep your chin up!" Keep scrolling.

I took my younger daughters skating one night as a Father/Daughter date. I didn't skate with them, but I did keep my eyes on the skating rink. One of the big topics on the news at that time was on racial division. I thought it was cool how color didn't matter out there as kids were making their rounds on their roller skates. As a kid would fall, like most kids do, someone, regardless of color, was there to help them back up. White, black, yellow... it didn't matter. All you saw were kids having fun and helping one another to keep balance and keep things going round in circles. This is how it should be in life. We're all on the same skating rink. If someone falls, be that person that helps them get back on track again. It just makes perfect sense.

Assertiveness

Being assertive lies somewhere between being overly agressive and lacking confidence and courage. It involves being bold and speaking up when necessary while being respectful of others. Here's what it means to be assertive:

- You can give an opinion or say how you feel.
- You can ask for what you want or need.
- You can disagree respectfully.
- You can offer your ideas and suggestions.
- You can say no without feeling guilty.
- You can speak up for someone else.

My kids are working on this characteristic and it's interesting because they all struggle with finding a balance. I have two kids that don't express themselves unless it's released through an argument, while the other two have no problems telling you what's on their minds even if it means hurting your feelings. For me, as a parent, I have to encourage communication, while at the same time, teach them to choose their words wisely. It can be difficult.

As adults, we have to learn good communication skills. When we are dealing with people, we should be assertive. People who speak assertively send the message that they believe in themselves. They're not too timid and they're not too pushy. They know that their feelings and ideas matter. They're confident.

People who are assertive tend to make friends more easily. They communicate in a way that respects other people's needs as well as their own. They tend to be better at working out conflicts and disagreements. People who give respect get respect in return.

Humility

There is a very important balance between having positive self-esteem and remaining humble that all kids and adults need to learn. In today's world where parents put a lot of emphasis on praising their children, it can be a challenge to make sure that kids still have humility. Back in my day, we earned our trophies. This generation gets them just for participating. Kids who lack humility may grow up to be arrogant adults, and no one wants that.

I DIDN'T SHOW UP TO PRACTISES. I DIDN'T SHOW UP FOR THE GAMES. BUT,... I GOT A TROPHY!

Humility can work well with confidence and positive self-esteem because when a child is self-assured and does not feel inferior to others, he won't feel the need to brag about his talents and achievements. Teaching humility to children begins with being an example and showing it ourselves. Parents should admit when they've made a mistake or don't know the answer and be willing to give credit to others. Then they can encourage kids to do the same.

STAY HUMBLE.

JOB APPLICATION

XYZ CO.

NOW THAT I'M A CERTIFIED ENGINEER.... SHOULD I GO AHEAD AND REQUEST A COMPANY-FURNISHED VEHICLE AND HOUSING TO GO ALONG WITH THE SIX-DIGIT SALARY?

An experience that comes to mind is when my son received his degree in Electrical Engineering. It was a proud moment for the both of us. He entered the working world with a feeling of pride that made him feel like he deserved the best job title with the best pay and nothing else would do. He learned quickly that this mindset will leave you jobless and living at home in a basement for a few years. He learned the value of humility and humbleness. He goes to work now with a different outlook on life and is doing well. This makes me proud.

Confidence

It's OK to have positive self-esteem. We should all feel good about ourselves. Actually, as parents, we should make a big deal when our kids achieve goals and reward positive behavior. This builds their confidence. I believe confidence can

YAY!

WELL, JOHNNY... SINCE YOU ALMOST DID YOUR CHORES,.... AND YOU ALMOST MADE GOOD GRADES IN SCHOOL,.... I THINK YOU DESERVE A BIG BOWL OF ICE CREAM WITH SPRINKLES.

MOM

lead to their happiness and we want our kids to grow into happy adults. Right?

However, we can overdo it. That's right! Excessive praise and neglecting discipline when they do wrong isn't good for their well being. Kids need to learn to win and they need to learn to lose, too. Getting a trophy or a gold star for participation isn't good when the kid really didn't do their best. They will grow up thinking that they don't have to try to achieve. They will feel like everything should be handed to them. Sadly, that's what's wrong with a lot of adults today.

You can gain confidence through failure as long as you don't quit. Believe in yourself. Set goals. Try and try again until you achieve your goal. This will develop patience and endurance. These are things you will definitely need when you are older.

Men As Husbands And Fathers According To The Bible

Role of the Husband in the Bible – Leader
The role of the husband according to the Bible starts with leadership. The scriptures make it pretty clear that a husband should be a leader of his home and have healthy control of his life.

For if a man know not how to rule his own house, how shall he take care of the church of God? - 1 Timothy 3: 5

Wives, submit yourselves unto your own husbands, as unto the Lord. For the husband is the head of the wife, even as Christ is the head of the church: and he is the saviour of the body. Therefore as the church is subject unto Christ, so let the wives be to their own husbands in every thing. - Ephesians 5: 22-24

But I would have you know, that the head of every man is Christ; and the head of the woman is the man; and the head of Christ is God. - 1 Corinthians 11: 3

One of the main roles of a husband according to the Bible is to lead. Leadership simply means to influence, so a biblically-based husband should influence his family. Husbands are not dictators. They should not make demands or rule over their wives. Instead, husbands should influence their wives and families according to what the Bible teaches. They should be examples, with their voice and their actions, that bring glory to God and value to their spouse and family. The fruit of a good biblically-based husband is a strong, confident, spiritually mature wife and family.

Two very specific ways a husband influences his home is through his provision and protection.

Role of the Husband in the Bible – Provider and Protector
The role of the husband according to the Bible starts with leadership and evolves around provision and protection. A husband will never influence his wife if he doesn't care for her. He can make demands and she may follow, but he will never truly have her heart unless he provides for her needs, cares for her well-being and protects her both physically and spiritually.

But if any provide not for his own, and specially for those of his own house, he hath denied the faith, and is worse than an infidel. - 1 Timothy 5: 8

Husbands, love your wives, and be not bitter against them. - Colossians 3: 19

Likewise, ye husbands, dwell with them according to knowledge, giving honour unto the wife, as unto the weaker vessel, and as being heirs together of the grace of life; that your prayers be not hindered. - 1 Peter 3: 7

God loves His daughters and the children they bear. When He gives one of His daughters to a man, He desires that the man takes care of her. Nowhere in the Bible does it teach that women and children should be considered second rate or inferior to men. Instead, He finds them so precious that He asks for special care to be given to them. It's a care that only biblically-based men can provide. Women are very capable of taking care of themselves — by themselves. However, God did make men and women different, and due to the physical nature and strength God gave men, He has given them the job of providing and protecting their families.

The physical nature and strength of a man is to be managed with grace and gentleness. God did not create men to lord over women nor did He create women to simply wait on men. He made them both to complement each other through healthy companionship.

Role of the Husband in the Bible – Companion

Husbands, love your wives, even as Christ also loved the church, and gave himself for it; That he might sanctify and cleanse it with the washing of water by the word, That he might present it to himself a glorious church, not having spot, or wrinkle, or any such thing; but that it should be holy and without blemish. So ought men to love their wives as their own bodies. He that loveth his wife loveth himself. For no man ever yet hated his own flesh; but nourisheth and cherisheth it, even as the Lord the church: For we are members of his body, of his flesh, and of his bones. For this cause shall a man leave his father and mother, and shall be joined unto his wife, and they two shall be one flesh. This is a great mystery: but I speak concerning Christ and the church. Nevertheless let every one of you in particular so love his wife even as himself; and the wife see that she reverence her husband. - Ephesians 5: 25-33

The role of the husband in the Bible is fulfilled through the heart of companionship. After all, no one ever hated his own body, but he feeds and cares for it, just as Christ does the church. We are members of his body.

THANKS, GOD! SHE'S HOT!

EVE

CENSORED

The relationship between a husband and a wife is meant to be one of love, respect and support. They are to help each other. This idea is introduced

185

at the beginning of the Bible in the story of the creation of Eve. Adam needed a companion and a suitable helper. So, God created Eve.

And Adam gave names to all cattle, and to the fowl of the air, and to every beast of the field; but for Adam there was not found an help meet for him. And the LORD God caused a deep sleep to fall upon Adam, and he slept: and he took one of his ribs, and closed up the flesh instead thereof; And the rib, which the LORD God had taken from man, made he a woman, and brought her unto the man. And Adam said, This is now bone of my bones, and flesh of my flesh: she shall be called Woman, because she was taken out of Man. Therefore shall a man leave his father and his mother, and shall cleave unto his wife: and they shall be one flesh. - Genesis 2: 20-24

This also leads to another understanding of companionship. God created men and women with natural, physical and emotional differences. Usually where one is weak, the other is strong. Because of this, a husband and wife can help each other by meeting the other person's needs through physical and emotional intimacy.

Nevertheless, to avoid fornication, let every man have his own wife, and let every woman have her own husband. Let the husband render unto the wife due benevolence: and likewise also the wife unto the husband. The wife hath not power of her own body, but the husband: and likewise

also the husband hath not power of his own body, but the wife. Defraud ye not one the other, except it be with consent for a time, that ye may give yourselves to fasting and prayer; and come together again, that Satan tempt you not for your incontinency. - 1 Corinthians 7: 2-5

When the needs of our spouse are properly met through healthy companionship, the two can help each other and can live a successful life together.

Through their companionship a husband and wife work together as a team to develop and grow a family. God's plan was that every home operate under the specific roles of both a husband and a wife and that through this they raise healthy children who honor God with their lives.

Children, obey your parents in the Lord: for this is right. Honour thy father and mother; (which is the first commandment with promise;) That it may be well with thee, and thou mayest live long on the earth. - Ephesians 6: 1-3

Children are blessed through the honor of their mother and father working in unison to train them up in the way they should go.

The companionship between a man and a woman is

directed by the influence of the husband through his provision and protection and is covered by his caring, gentle and graceful love for his wife and family. Without the biblical roles of a husband being fulfilled by a strong man of God, the family unit risks the difficulties brought on by sin and spiritual distortion. Satan desires the destruction of the family, but through Christ and proper understanding of biblical roles, the family is a strong and safe place to grow in God.

What Our Friends Are Saying

When I write a book, I like to get other people involved. I will ask them questions to get their point of view on the subject. If you listen, many times you will gain some knowledge and learn things you may not have even known before.

We asked our friends recently on Facebook, "What characteristics do you feel the male species should have to be considered a MAN?" Out of the ones that replied, here are there answers:

If you are man enough to make a child, be man enough to take care of it. - Ben Smith

A man can tell you he was wrong. That he did wrong. That he planned to. He can tell you when he is lost. He can apologize, even if sometimes it's just to put an end to the bickering. To put it simply, he steps up to the plate. With all things. He owns up with children, marriage, work. He does his best to be the best and take care of his own. He protects and loves. - Becca Todd

Always respect momma and daddy. Respect, love, feed, cloth and shelter your family. - Todd Smith

Responsible, respect for self and others, trustworthy, empathetic and loving – Debbie Fambro

A real man loves God. He works every day and is always on time. He will not let anyone mess with his woman, his children and his home... or the family dog. And a real man will never ever hit his woman for any reason. - Bobby Boyd

To be able to fix things - be it with duct tape or philosophical experience. Change a tire! - Tony Knott

A man should love his momma, treat her with respect and take care of her in her golden years. The way a man loves his momma will be the way he loves his wife and will be how he treats his family. He needs to love God above all and pray for his family daily. He also needs time to himself; to be able to relax his mind, to have fun doing his own projects and hobbies without fuss from his spouse. He needs to teach his sons how to be a loving husband, a hard worker, but to work smart. He needs to show his daughters that she is a princess and to teach her to wait for her one and only prince. Above all he needs to love himself and have confidence in himself. - Frances Todd

Responsible, integrity, protective. He puts God first and leads his family accordingly. - Lisa Brown

Have an instinctive need to own a truck.
Look at women's butts (all women)
Have an understanding that fishing is therapy
Watch out for the babies, even if they are not his own.
Lastly, always love mama (that includes his wife)
- David Dupree

Commitment, integrity, honesty, consistency, and humility. Of course, these make a woman, too. I think these are the qualities that show maturity. These make relationships last and make us capable of true intimacy. - Kathy Clark

If he has girls he must be able to fix their hair! Pony tails or braids or just plain brushing. He also should demonstrate how a man is supposed to love and treat them by the way he treats their mother! If he has sons, same thing except for the braids and pony tails! - Cindy Horsley

A man should always honor his parents, cherish his wife, protect his family and home, work hard, play hard, and stay faithful to his wife, family, and God. - Ted Richey

Always keep rope in the bedroom and duck tape. LOL – Jerrell Slack, Jr

The ability to listen... and not talk. - Allison Knott

The ability to admit when he is wrong. The ability to be the "head of his household" but do so from a position of respect, love and not strength/power. And most importantly... the ability to "push through the pain" and still bring home the bacon. - Greg Mims

Caring and respectful. - Donna Mosher

The ability to find your destination without asking for directions... iregardless of how long it takes. And yes... "iregardless" is a word. - Scott Kimbrell

To realize that he should give highest respect to his wife and family and put their needs above his. To want and strive to be the man God has meant for him to be. Love his wife & children as Christ loves His church. - Linda Shierling

Always have your priorities in line. God, your wife, your children, your job, then everything else. Don't let life steer you away from God's calling on your life. Remembering important dates such as anniversaries, birthdays, and holidays. Don't always expect the wife to shop, plan and execute these special days. Sometimes it's nice to not be the only one planning these things. - Frances Todd

I often tell my boys, "Be strong, but be kind." - Scott Thompson

Live your life so others will see and desire to also know God our Father through the way you live each day and hour and minute. - Theo Hankerson

Duty and honor, first to God, then to his family. - Karla Johns

The World's Version Of
The Man Code
(Extremely Condensed, Censored and Edited)

Internet: Searching For The Man Code

I saved this portion of the book for last because it is for entertainment purposes only. It really has no value whatsoever, other than a laugh or mere smirk. Here's why.

I did some research on the Internet to see if there is actually a 'man code' in place. It seems everyone has some ideas as to what codes a man should live by. I listed the ones I thought were funny. Amazingly, some of these man codes have a little bit of truth in them.

These are categorized for your convenience. I also had to edit and omit many of them due to their language. This is just for fun and doesn't reflect my own personal beliefs and thoughts. If you find any of this offensive, I apologize. Actually, if you think you might get offended or you are very sensitive about things, please stop reading now. Please note that you've been warned.

Entertainment: Movies

Movie Diet
A man's movie diet will contain at least one of the following

movies every two weeks:

Sports
Action
Comedy

If there isn't a movie for one of these categories, compensate by seeing a second action movie. If you don't like comedy or sports movies, deal with it. You're supposed to be a man.

Chick Flicks – The Commodities Exchange

A man shall only watch a chick flick in the presence of a woman. This is a commodities exchange: the man's boredom for the woman's cuddling. No man should be subject to endure *The Notebook.*

Chick Flicks – The Fair Trade

A man shall require his woman to see one action movie for every chick flick she requires of him.

Crying

A man may not cry openly at any movie.

Exception: A single tear may be shed if in relation to the death of a small and loyal companion. Example: Old Yeller, small child, a midget (it must be a ninja midget or midget of equal awesome value), etc.

Movie Law

When two guys go to see an awesome movie together, they must respect the safety seat rule. That rule is, there should be at least one empty 'safety' seat between each man to prevent incidental touching and allow maximum roll-out space.

Indications of a Manly Film - Doorknobs

Doorknobs are an invention to make opening doors easier for women and children. In manly films, a door can only be opened with:

- a kick/headbutt/flying kick
- a weapon, preferably of the shotgun variety
- a manly vehicle
- a thrown body

Indications of a Manly Film - Vehicles

A real man can operate any vehicle by instincts, no matter how obscure. Examples include semis, Harrier attack fighters, or any construction vehicles such as a crane or backhoe. This vehicle must be of the manly variety, preferably with dirt attached.

Indications of a Manly Film - Guns

There will be guns. Blades are acceptable, however dismemberment must occur.

Note: Women wielding guns does not count. A woman with a gun is like a woman driving a car, only a gun is a quicker death.

197

Entertainment: Music

Show Tunes

May it be noted: Only under realistic death threats, when the weapon of choice is held at the ready, may a man sing any show tune from any musical. With the exception of rock musicals such as *Across The Universe*. All the songs in said musical are originally by the Beatles.

'Man, I Feel Like a Woman' by Shania Twain

Any man caught lip-synching, singing, dancing to, or otherwise exulting in this song shall immediately lose his Man Card. Permanently.

Entertainment: Sports

Hula Hooping

No man shall ever hula hoop.

Women's Sports

Aerobics and cheerleading are not active sports, but are spectator sports. A man shall not spectate any women's sport, unless one of the following exceptions is met:

- if it furthers a relationship with a woman player
- if it furthers a relationship with a woman spectator

- if the man's daughter is a player
- three words: women's beach volleyball

Manly Sports

The following sports are considered manly, and you as a man should be able to completely explain the rules of two or more of the following:

- Football
- Boxing
- Cycling (try telling yourself it is not manly when trying to climb a mountain on a bicycle)
- Motocross
- NASCAR
- Formula 1
- Rally Driving
- Rowing (the only sport that originated as capital punishment)
- Lacrosse
- Rugby
- Basketball
- Curling
- Hockey
- Hunting*
- Hurling
- Shinty
- Rock Climbing

- Powerlifting
- Strongman
- Olympic Lifting
- Baseball
- Fencing

Hunting is not a sport in the traditional sense. However, that does not make it any less manly. Almost anything can be made manly if a gun is used and something dies (Note: That is not somebody).

Dancing Is Not a Sport

Besides dance fighting and break dancing, due to their suggestively violent names (they are exceptions to the following rule). Dancing is not a sport, case closed. Dancing is a fake sport for feminists.

Entertainment: Television

Changing the Channel

Changing the channel while sports are on is not allowed except to see the score of another game.

Channel surfing is mandatory during commercials. Commercials during games must be changed to another game (until the main game is back on) or can be muted (as an alternative) to complain about how crappy your team is. It must be with another man and he must agree with you. If he does not, you hold the right to remove him from your house. Complaining alone is whining.

Off limits TV shows:
- *Gossip Girl*

- *Oprah*
- *Days of Our Lives*
- *The View*
- Anything on Lifetime
- Men's Figure Skating (unless it's the movie, *Blades of Glory,* which is an 8 on the movie scale)
- *The Oxygen Network*
- *Passions* or any other soap opera
- Any interior design shows (exception: Do-It-Yourself specials on how to remodel your home into an advanced military fortress complete with an armory, moats, trenches, etc.)
- *The HGTV Network*
- *Gilmore Girls*
- *Sex and the City*

Stand-up Comedy

Men have the gift of a sense of humor and the gift of being able to appreciate things that are funny. This is a rare trait in women and no where is this more evident than during stand-up comedy. Male performers will often leave audiences anywhere from chuckling to rolling in the aisles, while the average female merely leaves the audience fidgeting uncomfortably.

If a woman attempts to be funny but is not, you are obligated to inform her.

Entertainment: Video Games

Game Choice

Every man must own at least one copy of a sports game, whether it is Madden, Mario Kart, FIFA, or something similar.

First-Person-Shooters are also a recommended addition to a man's library.

Any next-gen console is recommended, however, do not neglect the classics. The games you grew up on are still better than a lot of the crap that comes out these days.

Any well named World War 2 game is also acceptable. Nazis are not cool.

As a general rule of thumb, if there are guns, swords, explosions, scantily-clad women, or ninjas in a video game, it's worth playing.

Arcade Machines

All arcade machines are fair game with very few restrictions. If located in a public area, it is also acceptable to brag about winning. If challenged to a match on an arcade machine, and you lose, it is acceptable for up to ONE rematch to be called by a the loser. If it is a 2 out of 3 match, no rematches can be called.

Online Chatting

It is acceptable to decline a challenge with two exceptions: Air Hockey and shooting games.

In such online environments, as XBox Live, etc., conversation will be kept strictly to relevant topics such as enemy positions and insulting or 'chirping' opponents. No one wants to hear about your day or where you live.

Multiplayer

When playing a game against another man, it is considered unethical to glance at the section of screen controlled by another player. If voted guilty by the majority of the other players, it is perfectly acceptable to 'gang up' and kill the cheater's character.

When playing a game with people in the same room, if you unplug someone else's controller in order to kill them to break their spree, you should be dragged into the street and shot.

When playing man versus woman, assuming the woman is a potential or current date, the man is to keep the score close. He may win, but may not make it obvious that he is intentionally letting her take points as to make it seem like he is at her level. Exceptions include any time a woman is better at a game than a man, then the gloves are off. Give it your best shot.

Pokeman = Pokemon
Pokemon is a children's game.

Relationships: Dating

Friend Zone
Often after a length of time, a girl whom you may have an interest in will display that you are her friend. If it is clearly stated that you are her friend, a man shall move on. The friend zone is purgatory, or in some cases, sheer agony with little chance of escape.

Standard Creepiness Rule (Rule of Seven)
If a man dates a woman younger than (his_age / 2 + 7), while it is not forbidden, dating a woman who would be in violation of this rule is ill-advised. Furthermore, no man should date a woman over twice his age, minus 14.

DATE NIGHT.

NURSING HOME

Taken So Leave It
If a woman is taken, no man who does not claim the title of 'Her Man' may spend time alone with her. The title of 'Her Man' may only be given by the aforementioned woman. If it is found that she has more than one 'Man', all titles are null and void, and it is considered bad form to continue to spend time with her.

Second Best
No man shall settle for second best in a relationship with a woman. (i.e., the woman would rather be dating someone else but decides to 'settle' for you.) Upon finding out on his second best status, a man has one month to take the lead. If this goal cannot be met, he must put an end to the relationship. This rule is only void if the woman in question ranks an 8 or above.

Bros Before Hoes
No man may deny his friends, in order to spend time with any woman. This is by far the most important rule of the man laws and must be obeyed.

Hinderance
In any situation where a man's chance of success with a chick is diminished by another man's presence, the secondary male or 'third wheel' must leave at the earliest opportune moment.

The Friend's Ex - Rule 12
A man shall not date, hang out with, or friend request a fellow friend's ex. Man is required to ask said friend for permission to date or communicate with said ex, and if friend says yes, do so with his terms.

Sacrificing Manliness
No man shall sacrifice manliness to cater to a woman. If she

wanted a woman, she would date a woman. Examples of sacrificing manliness include:

- Claiming to like the movie, *Sweet Home Alabama*
- Listening to Backstreet Boys
- Crying
- Cuddling (unless it leads to more "hooking-up" in less than one-half hour.)

Exception: If outcome includes hooking up, any violation is void due to strategic move.

The Nice Guy
93.75% of nice guys never win. Of course this is referring to women. Nice guys often kick your butt on World of Warcraft to get back at you. Needless to say, the 6.25% of nice guys that do win often keep the girl.

Dating Your Ex-Girlfriend's Friends
While you were dating your ex-girlfriend, chances are that you had the opportunity to get to know her friends and even form your own relationship with them. At the conclusion of your relationship you may be tempted to enter into a relationship with a friend of your ex-girlfriend. If you dumped her, dating her friends is off-limits. If she dumped you, dating her friends is allowable, but proceed with caution.

Asking Out Via Text Message or Instant Message

No man shall ever attempt this, or do this. It will not work, and you'll seem like an unconfident princess. A man may get to know a woman better via texting or instant messaging but shall never ask said woman out via text message or instant message.

HOT LOOKING BRUNETTE I AM...
36-24-36... ROMANTIC WALKS ON
THE BEACH I LIKE.

CLICK!
CLICK!

CLICK!
CLICK!

Online Dating

Dating online is permissible, but no man shall admit to it.

A man shall be wary of the pictures posted on their date's profile. If she looks too hot to need online dating, she is probably ugly and/or fat. Rule of thumb: If an online girl is ranked 7+, it's not her real picture. If she's rated 9+, it's not a girl.

If a man has a six pack he is allowed one picture of his rock hard abs. Any more and it looks like he is compensating.

Cheating - Lame Excuses

A man should not cheat, but when he does he should do his best to escape the ramifications, as it is simple biological fact that man will do his best to maximize his genetic chances. Deny till you die!

The Breakup

No man should ever sacrifice manliness when breaking up with a woman. You break up face-to-face and tell her what was wrong with her, then its another guy's problem.

Acceptable Reasons

The following are acceptable reasons to dump a woman:

- She is a princess.
- She farts.
- She uses your toothbrush.
- She has a problem with your dog ravaging her leg and forces you to choose between her and Rex.

Over The Phone/Via E-mail Or A Letter

Breaking up with a girl over the phone is to be considered a cardinal sin against all that is manly. To appear that weak and scared of what the girl may do is not only emasculating, but downright rude. No man would shy away from a woman like that. It also spreads a bad reputation, which may damage chances with prospective hook-ups.

Relationships: Family

Baby Talk

When talking to a baby, men do not use baby talk, men use man talk.

Baby Feeding

Only the woman will feed the baby. Bottles are not good enough, so have her use the more natural ones.

Baby Training

At six months old, a man child shall begin training for professional sports. If he's old enough to crawl, he's old enough to crawl across an end zone with a football.

Treatment of Children

Spanking (not abuse) is acceptable to serve as a punishment for anything above petty mischief.

A man is not obliged, or even encouraged, to give 'TLC' to his children. What is acceptable, however, is to vaguely address the fact that there are shorter-than-average people running about the house.

Naming

A man should not give his son a name conventionally given to a girl. Gender nonspecific names such as Pat, Kris and Erin should also be avoided.

So-called creative spellings of names are not acceptable names for men. Examples of such spelling alternatives include the exchange of the -ey suffix for -eigh, and the misuse of the letter Y (as in Alyx). Just because Lynyrd Skynyrd did it doesn't mean you can, too.

A man should not name his son after construction supplies, tools, weapons or other manly objects in an attempt to emphasize masculinity. These should instead be used as middle names.

Only one or two syllable car-related names may be used for nicknames (Dodge, is acceptable as is Chevy, while Oldsmobile is not). Also, foreign brands are not acceptable (Toyota, Hyundai, Mercedes-Benz, etc.) especially French brands (Peugeot, Renault, etc.); the exception is "MG," which is an acceptable coincidence if those are, in fact, the person's initials.

THIS IS MY SON, DEWALT. UMM... DEWALT CRAFTSMAN-MAKITA FERGUSON.

An example of a manly name is Johnson McCragrock. The first is hardy, but, an acceptable Christian name. Others include Brick, or Slate - building materials. The last name is not recognizable, yet betrays the idea of the man spending his free time breaking boards with his belt muscles. Any name that suggests that this child could grow up to be a warrior on a medieval battle field weilding a giant hammer is encouraged, such as 'Stonecrusher Lionheart' or 'Bonebreaker MacKillsallot'. Having last names such as 'Payne', 'Hurtz', etc. are awesome and imply power, physical damage and overall manliness. Thus, they should be utilized to create names of the aforementioned breed.

In some instances, it may be acceptable to name your child after a superhero, but only super heroes whose names are not in violation of previous rules, or use alliteration. Unacceptable examples include 'Peter Parker' or 'Oliver Queen'. Acceptable names include Logan, Clark, Bruce, nny variation of the Flash's names, or Captain America. Steve Rogers is also acceptable. The manliest name of this variety is 'Magneto Jones'.

Relationships: Friends

Bachelor Party
Any man who brings a camera to a bachelor party or bar hopping, in doing so, surrenders any right to life and lives further only at the mercy of other men.

Birthday
No man shall be required to buy a birthday present for another man. In fact, even remembering your buddy's birthday is strictly optional. However, should a man choose to buy a birthday present for another man, it does not affect his manliness positively or negatively.

Blood Brother
A man may come across someone in their life, a fellow man, with whom they share a sense of loyalty, commitment, and similar taste. This man may come to be one's 'Blood Brother', with

whom it is known that you will share any secret, any hardship, and every jail cell.

BLOOD BROTHERS

Flying Low

If a man's fly is down, that's his problem. You didn't see anything.

Sports

When picking players for sports teams, it is permissible to skip over your buddy in favor of better athletes - as long as you don't let him be the last person standing on the sideline.

Communication

When talking on the phone or in person to another man about sports, it is inpermissible to put the other man on hold for a call from a girlfriend, wife, or for any other matter, other than an exceptional business opportunity, in which case the other man will understand, provide you cut him in.

Conflict Resolution

In the event that two men disagree, the following are appropriate conflict resolution methods:

- Arm wrestling
- Thumb wrestling is not an acceptable alternative, since this requires prolonged hand-to-hand contact.
- FPS or sports video games
- Rock / Paper / Scissors

- Bare knuckle boxing
- Beer-pong tournament

The loser may call 'best 2 out of 3', but afterwards the decision is final.

High Fives

If two men are to high five each other and their hands miss, it is not permissible to attempt another high five. That would be comparable to holding hands. Said high five must be played off like they never happened.

Man Hugs (Mugs)

- Are to be done only with one arm
- Each other's face should not come within an inch and a half of each other
- Violently pat on back, but never exceed three pats
- Nearly break the other guy's rib cage
- Men do not linger
- NOT TO BE DONE FREQUENTLY

Man Touch

If man A touches man B in the crotch or buttocks, whether accidental or on purpose, man B is required to punch man A in the face.

Physique Comments

A man is to not comment on another mans physique of any kind, unless in the name of humor.

Friends and Relationships

Bros before hoes.

Girl "Dibs" Guideline

If a man expresses interest in a woman to his friends, he has dibs, or exclusive rights to her.

Prerequisites for said guy to call dibs:
- Said woman must know his name.
- Said woman be in his league.

Expiration Dibs are automatically broken if:
- Said woman shoots him down.
- A period of two weeks has passed without success.

Dibs cannot be called again by said man on said woman. At this point said friends have every right to call dibs on said woman.

AKA

This is also known as calling squirrel. They keyword squirrel is used so that the hunted female does not realize she has been targeted. Should another man target another man's squirrel, this is known as scamming on someone's squirrel. No man shall scam on another man's squirrel.

Wingman

A man is obligated to provide wingman services to guys who are good friends. The wingman's mission is to help the friend get hooked-up. A wingman is not allowed to discuss the mission, especially if it was a failure. Discussing a secret mission may result in forfeit of future wingman reciprocation and demotion of friend status.

Miscellaneous Relationship Rules

No man is allowed to make fun of or negatively comment on any other man's hookup, girlfriend, etc., unless he has previously been involved in some sort of relationship with her, thus insulting himself in the process.

THIS IS MY FRIEND... CARL.

YOUR SISTER IS SUPER FINE! IS SHE SINGLE?

If you've known a guy for more than 24 hours, his sister is off limits forever unless you intend to marry her. Dating is allowed IF and ONLY IF she is older than your friend, and is rated a 7 (on a scale of 1-10) by at least 3 other friends. In addition it is pre-requisite to have the 'talk' with said friend and gain approval before pursuing the sister.

Men do NOT give relationship advice to other men unless requested. Venting about a woman does NOT imply a request for relationship advice.

Honorary Manhood

Men do not recognize female friends. There are male friends and potential dates; that's it. Having said that, there are certain woman that have earned a place among men.

Qualifications

A woman qualifies for honorary manhood if she displays 2 out of 3 of the following:

- She is as competent as the guys at burping and farting.
- She consistently beats the guys at any man game.
- She engages in man talk fluently and often.

Implications

Honorary manhood has the following implications:

- All rights and responsibilities of the Man Code apply as if she were a man.
- Men don't flirt with other men, not even honorary ones.

Initiation

Honorary Manhood Initiation Methods:

- The woman being nominated for honorary manhood ("the nominee") can only be nominated by a real man ("the nominator").
- The nominee must participate in a drinking night in which she goes drink-for-drink with said nominator.
- The nominee must not hesitate, complain or pass out during said drinking.

- Puking is okay, as long as the nominee continues to drink thereafter, or immediately goes for a kebab.
- The nominee must defeat at least one real man at a male-ratified and refereed drinking game.
- If the nominator should decree the nominee to be worthy of the title of Honorary Manhood, he must ipso facto perform an unexpected, no-holds-barred, man-brawl headbutt to the nominee.
- If the nominee is able to receive said headbutt without falling to the floor, losing conciousness, crying, or displaying any other hints of weakness, her induction will be considered and decided upon by the presiding males.
- If the nominee returns said headbutt to her nominator in a manner which causes any presiding members to flinch, her induction is immediate and automatic.
- Alternatively, a no-holds barred wrestling match may be held between nominator and nominee, winner decided by knock-out or submission.
- Alcohol must be involved.

Relationships: Marriage

Anniversaries
An anniversary is recognized on a yearly basis, under no circumstances will anything be celebrated in an interval other than a year.

Surnames
No man shall assume the last name of his spouse.

Relationships: Pets

Cats

Women like cats. Men say they like cats. But when women aren't looking, men kick cats and replace them with baby lions. It is then acceptable to train the lions to attack on command, but be docile otherwise. A pet cat is only permissible when said cat is vicious, ill-tempered, and/or mangy. Kittens are never manly pets.

Dogs

A man shall have a dog. Dogs are the 'men' of the animal kingdom. Even a female dog is more of a 'man' than a cat. It is acceptable for a man to own a cat in addition to a dog if the purpose of the cat is to amuse the dog and to serve as a potential meal in an emergency.

TLC

A man shall love his dog. Therefore, the phrase 'I love you' is perfectly acceptable to say to a dog, even when in front of another man. Baby talk such as 'Who's a good puppy?' DOES NOT get the same exemption as 'I love you'. It is acceptable for a man to play with his dog, though preferably by wrestling or other exhibition of dominance behavior.

WHAT IS THAT?

IT'S PRECIOUS.

Miniature

A man shall never own a dog which is smaller than an average house cat, and shall never under any circumstances adorn a dog with ribbons, or bows, or 'doggie' sweaters.

Names

A man shall only give a dog a cute name, such as "Buttons" or "Fluffy," in an ironic sense. The dog must be of an exceptionally manly breed such as a Rottweiler or a Doberman to merit such a name.

Neutering

Neutering a male dog is unacceptable, as is spaying a female. If forced to, avoid all eye contact with the animal while on the way to, or at, the veterinarian's clinic for the procedure.

Other Pets

There are other animals (non-canonical) which may be considered manly enough to own. These animals include:

- Pigs
- Horses (NOTE: MUST be a HORSE--not a PONY--in addition, it must be trained in combat or jousting, and even then, only ONE horse)
- Scorpions
- Grizzly bears
- Gators
- Large predatory cats

- Great white sharks
- Giant squids
- Wolves (essentially more vicious dogs)
- Elephants (if trained in combat, then referred to as War Mammoths)

Note: Many horses/ponies are allowed and still manly if you are on or own a ranch/farm.

Monkeys

These naturally gentle apes must be bred for war and subservience. If your ape companion may be mistaken for a small hairy soldier, then he is ready to be a man pet. If said ape can kill quieter than Solid Snake, then the ape may be an Honorary Man, with all rights and responsibilities thereof. If he flings his own feces at lesser men, all the better.

Ferrets

A ferret may be considered as a pet only if you train it to attack cats and men who violate vital man rules. As ferrets are naturally mean and violent creatures, they are a suitable for apartments that are too small for a dog.

Style: Accessories

Belts

A man's belt must match his shoes.

Murse

No man shall carry a man bag. A normal size wallet should hold everything you need.

Jewelry

No man shall wear jewelry besides a watch and wedding ring.

Style: Clothing

How To Dress
A man shall go into his shorts drawer and take the TOP pair of shorts and put them on. He shall then proceed to the shirt drawer and don TOP shirt. There will be no 'matching' under any circumstances. If challenged on his mismatched clothes or horrid color combinations, it is appropriate to punch that person.

You LOOK
STUPID!

FASHION
CRITIC

Shorts
'Coach' shorts are only to be worn by the 50+ crowd and ONLY if they are ACTUAL coaches. Cutoffs are for kids and hippies. Kids get a pass, hippies get a beating. Under no circumstances may any man wear capri shorts.

Fedora
Nice choice! If its good enough for Indiana Jones, its good enough for you. I mean, can YOU outrun a giant boulder and tribals with blow darts?

Baseball Caps and/or Trucker Hats
These may be worn. However, under no circumstances shall a man ever wear them with the bill at any angle other than 0

degrees or 180 degrees whereas his direct frontal line of sight (in a straight line) is 0 degrees.

Pants - Length
The bottom of a man's pants must be no higher than 3 inches from the ground and no lower than 1 inch.

Pants - Bagginess
If you are not a rapper, and you do not live in the ghetto, you will not wear sagging or baggy pants at any time.

Shirt Without Pants
No man shall wear a shirt without pants... ever. Pants must be the first item worn by man at the start of his day, and the last item to come off. (The exception to the latter part of this rule is if the man sleeps in the nude, in which case his boxers are to be the first and last things worn.)

Kilt
This is the only manly skirt. Only the Scottish may wear these. The only 2 exceptions to this rule are for themed proms/frat parties, and dedicated Curlers. As the true gentleman's sport is curling and to wear a kilt in doing such sport is considered manly.

Suspenders

Suspenders are frowned upon by the male community as they have been largely replaced by belts. If worn, suspenders must support the wearers pants. If they are left hanging down to be used as a 'fashion' statement, they may be forcefully removed. Firemen and any other manly profession (such as fisherman) may wear suspenders as they please.

'Girl' Pants/Jeans

Commonly seen in the 'emo' subculture of the 'punk' subculture of the Gothic culture. A man shall never, ever wear pants, or any other article of clothing for that matter, belonging to the opposite sex. Man caught wearing these is automaticaly considered a princess and gay.

Shirts - Pink Shirts

No man shall wear pink! Real men do not trust pink t-shirts that say 'Real Men Wear Pink'. This is like trusting Garth Brooks that country music is good, or Jeffrey Dahmer that humans are tasty. Men who wear pink have an agenda and are not to be trusted.

Shirts - Tucked in

No man shall tuck in a shirt without buttons. This is a law in 32 states and all of Canada and Europe. Exceptions to this rule are while participating in a sporting event, carrying a firearm in a belt holster or enduring extended periods of temperatures less than

15 degrees.

Top vs Shirt
No man shall ever refer to a 'shirt' as a 'top' unless said 'shirt' is a frilly open-chest garment on a woman.

Footwear - Dress Shoe Limit
No man shall own more than three pairs of dress shoes.

Footwear - Matching
A man should wear brown shoes with brown pants and black shoes with everything else.

Socks
At no time shall a man wear sandals with socks. Sandals are pushing it as it is.

YOU LOOK STUPID!

FASHION CRITIC

Formal Wear
If at all possible, most men should avoid any kind of function requiring formal dress. Exceptions are allowed if you are a classy, but still manly man. A classic, highly cliché example of such a man is James Bond.

Vests
No man shall wear a vest based on 'fashion'. Vests may be worn if the color is of the bright orange reflective variety, the vest is bullet proof, or if the vest is worn with a 3-piece suit.

Ties With Formal Wear

No man past the age of 15 shall ever wear a clip on tie as a part of a formal outfit. After reaching 13 years of age, a male shall begin the process of learning the art of tying the tie. Men may only have women tie their ties for them if they already know how to tie a tie, but do not feel like doing it themselves.

YOU LOOK STUPID!

FASHION CRITIC

Ties Without Formal Wear

Never shall a man wear a tie with a T-shirt. You are not an 'emo' rocker. 'Emo' is not manly.

Sport coat / Suit jacket

This shall be worn to a formal event, but it may be required that you remove it at a later time. Never shall a man's jacket have more than four buttons. You should look formal, but not like you're trying to hide. If you do, in fact, have something to hide, start working out.

Socks - Toe Socks

No man shall wear toe socks. It's worse than wearing women's underwear.

Socks - White Socks

Although fashion commentary is usually frowned upon, a man is required to mock a fellow man caught wearing white socks with dark dress pants.

Underwear - Commando
The absence of underwear (aka Commando) is not acceptable unless severe situations necessitate it. Or if you haven't done laundry in a while. Or if you're wearing a Kilt.

Style
A man shall be restricted to three genres of underwear: boxers, briefs, and a combination of the aforementioned.

Thong
Under no circumstance shall a man wear a thong or women's underwear, unless utilized as punishment for breaking man law.

YOU LOOK STUPID!

FASHION CRITIC

CENSORED

Clothes - Borrowing
No man shall borrow clothes from anyone ever. If you don't have a pair of heels that match your purse, go to the store and buy a pretty dress for yourself, too.

Clothes - Shopping
A man does not shop for clothes. A man must not browse, nor enter a clothing store unless he has a specific purpose for doing so.

Clothes - Garment Number
A man must never take more then three items to the change room at one point in time. A man that brings 2 or more items into a change room must buy all the items, no exceptions.

Clothes - Questions

When acquiring clothing a man will not ask if a garment makes him look fat. He will not ask for female opinion, nor will he let a female pick garments for him to 'just try on'. The only question a man may ask is, "Is this something a female would wear?" If the answer is yes, no matter how 'comfortable in his sexuality' the man may be, the garment must be discarded immediatly, ritual burning is an option for pink shirts and pastel colored pleated pants. However if the man has a hidden agenda behind bringing multiple pieces of clothing into a changing room in such a way that he gets a woman to come with this is acceptable.

Style: Hygiene

Beard
The beard is highly recommended. If it's good enough for Chuck Norris, it's good enough for you.

Facial Hair February
Facial Hair February is a long standing manly tradition, and every man is encouraged to participate. Shave your face clean on February 1st and then do not shave until March.

It is noted however, that this practice is popular in November as well being known as 'No Shave November'.

Moustache

With the exception of most police officers, there are three men who look good with only a moustache. Two of them are Burt Reynolds and Tom Selleck. You are not the third. Leave the moustache in the eighties where it belongs. The only exception to this tenet is the full handlebar, and even then is only allowable in its fully formed state.

FEBRUARY

MARCH

Grooming - Mirror Time

A man shall not spend more than two minutes in front of a mirror, unless said man is shaving. Shaving is a manly pursuit (aka Mansuit). Shaving in the shower saves time in front of the mirror.

Bathing

A man may have no more than four total bathroom elements: shampoo, conditioner if necessary, soap, and Lava soap. Washcloth is allowed. Loofahs and poofs are strictly off limits at all times. An exception occurs for GoJo or other similar grease removers that can be used in the shower, this is only allowed when Lava soap absolutely will not work. This exception is due to the fact that if you have enough grease on you to require GoJo you were obviously doing something manly.

Showering

While showering a man must spend a minimum of 80% of the time cleaning his genitals, 10% armpits, 7% hair (head) and the remainder cleaning his front upper torso. For the rest of the body, just being wet counts.

Head Hair - Long Hippie Hair

If a man has long hair, he shall also have facial hair. If a man is unable to grow facial hair, then he shall not have long hair. People should not have to wonder if a man is a guy or a chick.

Head Hair - Mullet

Mullets are only acceptable under the conditions that the party in the back is equal to or greater than the business in the front, and the mullet remains free of styling or haircare products of any kind. If the latter is present, immediate removal is recommended, or severe beating may result. Mullets are also not to come into contact with weak facial hair or females under any circumstances.

Head Hair - Afro

Afros are a true representation of greatness in a man. Only a scarce number of men can pull the afro off. Caucasians can very rarely pull this look off, as their hair wants to fall or go into extreme curls. Usually people of black decent are the ones to truly hold this honor. However, racially mixed individuals have a possibility to grow an afro, and when they do, they are usually considered the best example. Afros can be rarely seen on black women, which is a treat. Afros that sit on top of a mans head should be treated with respect.

Head Hair - Baldness

No man shall ever use a rug or any hair re-growth treatments. That is a sign of weakness. If man is balding on top, it is recomended that the rest of the head match. A shaved head is one of the most manly.

NICE FLOWING CURLS! SIMPLY FABULOUS!

ARG READERS

Head Hair - The Haircut Comment Clause

Men shall not comment on other men's haircuts unless radical alteration has taken place. Examples of radical alteration include; mullet to complete head shave, anchor man haircut to spiked Mohawk, standard hair to a buzz cut dyed in your team's colors. Commenting on less radical hair events are to be considered excessive attention to another man's appearance.

Exception: In event of a particularly well-done cut, one sentence is acceptable as a compliment to the barber by proxy. Example: "Nice haircut." No more. Leave it be.

Head Hair - Dyed Hair

In no way is dyed hair manly. Period. However, highlights are exceptable, but only in the event your barber is a woman.

Head Hair - Gingers

The second a ginger is born, he becomes a man, no questions asked.

Proven examples:
Rupert Grint, Ed Sheeran, Mick Hucknell, Gordon Ramsey and Lieutenant Horatio Caine, the king of one-liners.

Armpit Hair

With the exception of the entertainment industry or an organized combat event, no man should ever shave armpit hair. To do so is a display of feminism.

Eyebrow Plucking

A man shall pluck his eyebrow if and only if he is separating a unibrow into two distinct eyebrows, but said man shall not admit to plucking said eyebrow(s).

WHAT?

NO-OO!

ARG READERS

Leg Hair

Just as with armpit hair, this must never be shaved. Also, disagreements can be resolved by giving the choice to the person with the most leg hair. Exceptions are for sporting events, like swimming.

Shaving

A man WILL NOT shave another man. The only exceptions are:
- A professional barber using a cut-throat razor (and only a cut-throat).
- As punishment, a man can be forced to shave another man's back.
- If a man passed out drunk without finding the safety of a bed, his hair can be shaved away.
- Preparation prior to surgery, when there is not a female to do it.

Work and Leisure: Behavior

Forbidden
Men are not allowed to say the following expressions:
- You hurt my feelings.
- I'm lost. Can you give me directions?
- Did you see Brokeback Mountain?
- I've had enough beer.
- No thanks, I'm vegan.
- Where do you see this relationship going?
- I'm too tired to gamble.
- This food is too spicy.
- Do I look fat in this?

Expletives
Swearing when around other men is acceptable, swearing in the presence of women is NOT acceptable unless they are in the Navy or the setting is a professional or collegiate sporting event.

Feelings
Men have feelings too. This being said, men do not 'talk about their feelings'. Men have feelings same as men have nipples. Both are useless. If you whine like Fallout Boy, be prepared to give milk on command.

Work and Leisure: DIY

Honey-Do List
If a man waits less than two weeks before fixing something after being asked, he is whipped.

Manly Job
A man shall only attempt to mend or make something when

there is a less than manly job to be done, such as feeding baby or washing dishes.

Efficiency
You have not made any mistake if you find that there are extra pieces after reassembling or assembling an object. In fact, you have just found a way to make that object more efficient.

Improvements
A man will not only repair a fault, but will attempt to upgrade the original item that was broken. The greater the improvement, the more of a man he is. For example, repairing your grandmothers electric scooter and building in rocket power and automatic weapons is completely acceptable.

YEAH, BUT... THINK OF THE MONEY WE'LL SAVE ON TOILET PAPER.

DIY CRITIC

Professional Assistance
A man will NEVER hire a professional trade worker to do work in his own home. Every man is genetically equipped with the ability to perform plumbing, electrical, and general housing repairs at birth. Should a man not be able to fix a set problem, the fault quite obviously rests with the tools he is using, or any female that is watching. Exception, when a man is intentionally being lazy.

Manly Equipment

If it moves and it shouldn't, use duct-tape on it. If it doesn't move and it should, use WD-40 on it. This rule applies to any and all objects that need mending or fixing. Exception, Fans. (WD-40 breaks fans)

Crying - Acceptable

It is OK for a man to cry ONLY under the following circumstances:

- When a heroic dog dies to save its master.
- After wrecking your boss's car. (these are often tears of laughter)
- Actually seeing Chuck Norris execute a roundhouse kick in real life.
- One hour, 12 minutes, 37 seconds into "The Crying Game".
- When Arnie is lowered into the metal at the end of T2, a single tear may roll down your face.
- When struck in the testicles by an object with considerable force. His friends are also allowed to cry with laughter.
- When a soldier gives his life for his people and country.

Gym Etiquette - Gym Faux Pas

Phrases that may NOT be uttered to another man while lifting weights:

- "Yeah, Baby, Push it!"
- "C'mon, give me one more! Harder!"
- "Another set, and we can hit the showers!"
- "Your muscles are just soooo big."

Gym Etiquette - Locker Room Gaze
In locker rooms, men shall practice the unfocused 'seeing without looking' gaze, enabling them to see where they are going without actually looking at anyone else. Walking around nude in the locker room is wrong! Wear a towel.

Gym Etiquette - Shower Faux Pas
Phrases that may NOT be uttered to another man in or near the showers:
- "Is there room for one more in here?"
- "I dropped the soap."
- Anything other than a story about manly conquests.
- "Can you reach this spot on my back?"

Cleaning
Men are required to clean organic particulate matter from areas which may come into contact with human skin in the near future, within their own domiciles. A magazine on the coffee table is not life threatening, even if it remains after the apocalypse. Men don't dust, nor will they clean the kitchen.

Phone
A man must never talk to another man on the phone for more than five minutes, unless he is being guided through the bomb defusing process in a hijacked orphanage/office building.

Dancing
Most forms of dancing are unmanly, and any man dancing can be called a princess ONCE. Drunken jigs are acceptable however.

(bonus points if you can dance better drunk than sober)

Jobs

All men must aspire to have a manly job, and all men with manly jobs are permitted to look down on those without manly jobs regardless of pay or status. The following jobs are considered manly:

- Assassin
- Astronaut
- Barman
- Builder
- Chefs (Professional chefs, working at Burger King does not count)
- Firefighter
- Geologist
- Gunsmith
- Gynacologist
- Hunter
- Lumberjack
- Marine
- Martial Arts Instructor
- Mechanic
- Mercenary
- Women's Fitness Instructor
- Pilot
- Policeman
- Professional Sportsman

- Roadie
- Sailor
- Secret Agent
- Soldier
- Video games tester
- Any job in the military other than secretaries and nurses

Work and Leisure: Food and Drink

Saliva

No man shall ever eat or drink after another man. If there is any possibility of saliva exchange, it is practically kissing.

Exception 1: For the sake of shots, 80 proof liquor is proven to kill man germs and is therefore allowed under man rules. Anything below 80 proof is not safe, but if it's below 80 proof, and it isn't beer, it doesn't belong in a man's glass, bottle or can.

Exception 2: When participating in partial & full contact sports, accidental sharing is permitted.

Can Crushing

Crushing a can on your head was once a manly act, but the practice started back when beer cans were made of steel. Such an act required a forehead as tough as an anvil and triceps as big as a small child. (Our hats are off to you, Mr. Belushi.) Now, since cans are made from aluminum, any yahoo can perform this seemingly masculine act. Therefore, the can crushing has been banned from being a manly act. This rule does not apply to unopened cans.

Drink Colors

There are only two acceptable colors for what a man is drinking:

- Clear, as in Gin & Tonic, Vodka Tonic, Martinis.
- Brown, as in Bourbon, Scotch, Whiskey and Beer.

Only exceptions to this rule is under demonstration or challenge to manliness in which additives are added such as habanero sauce or snake venom.

Last Beer/Pizza

If you didn't bring it, and you didn't ask, don't touch it. Save the last for the guy who paid for it.

Six-Pack

If you compliment a guy on his six-pack, you'd better be talking about his choice of beer. Unless the man is Chuck Norris, and you want to get on his good side.

Fruity

It is permissible to drink a fruity alcohol drink only when you're sunning on a tropical beach... and it's delivered by a topless model and only when it's free.

Meat

Meat is the primary source of sustenance for a man, and at no time will said man consume any type of meat substitute, such as Tofu or a Veggie-burger, or else bear the pseudonym Princess. Meat must come from a beast, and if at all possible, a beast from the wild. This does not indicate 'free-roaming cattle', this means a wild boar. (Note: any man converting to a vegetarian for ANY REASON shall also bear the pseudonym princess.) Unless of course the man is born or needs to practice being a vegetarian because of religion, such as some Hindus and Catholics during Lent. Also, a man may avoid meat for medical reasons such as if he is in a life-or-death situation because he is morbidly obese, but then again, if you had to go without meat, why would you want to keep living anyway?

Bacon

Possibly the manliest food available in a grocery environment, bacon is the staple of every meal. Do NOT grill bacon in the nude. A woman may cook bacon, unless the bacon is to be grilled. Men grill, women cook.

Steak

If it came from a cow and isn't ground into processed beef - it shall be steak - anything else is just odd. Deer steak, boar steak, salmon steak and the like are to be GRILLED from the wild i.e. you kill em' then grill em'

Note: steak is to be grilled. DO NOT LET A WOMAN NEAR THE BOVINE UNTIL IT IS GRILLED!

Hunting

Hunting must be attempted whenever available. If there is an elk in the backyard, do not pet it. Kill it with your bare hands. It is now dinner. However, using deer stands or anything else with an ease level comparable to self-aiming rifles makes you a Princess, as the name 'Hunting' implies you are to find your prey not wait on it, wuss.

Barbecuing

Women may not touch the grill – ever.

Exception: If the man grilling has died defending his food, the woman MUST save the steaks before grieving.

Grilling is essential to a man's way of life - it is the lifeblood of a meat-based diet. Do not wear an apron. Real men bathe in grease. Unless geographically limited, a man must attempt to grill with charcoal. A steak cooked more than medium-rare is a criminal act. Always buy high quality meats - even hamburger, so you can taste blood.

HOW DO YOU WANT YOUR STEAK?

ARG READERS

Fire

Remember, there is no meat without fire, and no fire without meat. S'mores are not to be eaten after burgers, if at all. Any fire for the purpose of decoration must exceed three feet in height, and be used as a warning flare for passing jets.

Propane

Propane is girly. Fire is a sacred tool to man. The exception to this rule is Hank Hill and only because he has spent his life following all other man-laws. Truly, if not for his obsession with Propane (and the unfortunate dog-dancing incident) he would be one of the Man Code's highest devotees.

Pizza

Never leave pizza unattended with a room full of drunk buddies. Period.

Salad

Salad is not food. Women, children, and rabbits eat salad. They need it to grow. If you are a real man, all you need to grow is a bigger beard. This rule can be lifted if the salad is over fifty percent meat (aka a Burger).

I'M HAW NGRY!

SALAD

ARG READERS AND/OR RABBITS

Putting Away Bread

After eating bread with the little plastic bag-crimper, do not put the crimper back on the bread bag. It is physically impossible for a man to do this. Spin the bread and tuck the flap under.

Slicing Bread

A man must use the largest, most dangerous knife at hand when slicing bread. Or anything sharp. A man will never use a bread slicer. Instead, if no knife or other sharp implement is at hand, he will rip said bread apart with his teeth.

Restaurant Etiquette - Ordering

While ordering at a restaurant, a man must be able to pronounce the food that he is ordering without asking for help of any kind. A man shall never order anything with an overly faux-European name, such as the Rooty Tooty Fresh and Fruity at IHOP. Save for attempting to look 'cultured' and 'suave' in the company of a suggestively-dressed woman.

Restaurant Etiquette - Decision Time

A man must not take longer than the woman to decide. We came to that restaurant to eat and NOT look over the menu. It is your job to hurry the woman along. If you are slow, do not use 'umm' 'uhh' or any other placeholder. The server will NOT walk away from you.

Eating

A man must eat with the utensils provided to him. It is not permissible to ask for a fork and spoon at a Chinese/Japanese restaurant (lest ye be called incompetent), and it is likewise not permissible to ask for a pair of chopsticks if fork/knife is the default (showoff). If there is any doubt, men are required to eat with their hands.

Food Etiquitte

If eating a popsicle in public, the man must bite the popsicle and not lick or suck. Same rule applies with bananas.

No man must eat a hotdog without a bun, unless it is to add more meat to chilli.

When drinking a drink out of a cup that accepts a lid, a lid is not to be used. Lids are for children. (Exception: When going through the drive through and eating in the car)

Cooking

A man doesn't cook, unless it's his job or he wants to impress a woman.

Work and Leisure: Restrooms

Conduct - Attendant

A man should tip the guy who hands you towels, and make appropriate conversation with him. A man should NOT buy any of the colognes or body sprays he is peddling.

Conduct - Seat Up

Always. Even after dropping logs.

Conduct - Talking

This is only allowed in the circumstances of all men in a conversation being in the same situation (i.e. all stood at urinal or all waiting to get a urinal). Should a change in status occur for any member of the conversation, that man must leave the conversation immediately. If a conversation is taking place at a urinal, all men must face forwards and stare at the wall in front of them, nowhere else. Silence must be observed at all times whilst in a cubicle, groans are allowed, however.

Note: If the conversation takes place at the urinals and ends in mutual agreement, never offer to 'shake on it'.

Urinals - Eye Position

Eyes forward at the urinal, Susie. There's no reason to be looking around in the men's room. Get in, do your business, and get out. Looking straight down at your own johnson is permissible, especially when aiming for things inside the urinal. You can also look up, but that just looks stupid.

Urinals - Splash Zone (One Man Rule)

No man shall occupy a urinal immediately adjacent to another man. If there are no suitable urinals, a line shall be formed.

Bathrooms in sports stadiums are an exception, where all urinals are fully occupied (and usually accompanied by long lines for each) but not separated by walls.

Two Jiggle Rule
If you jiggle more than twice, you're playing with it.

Urinate Standing
A man shall not urinate sitting down unless also dropping logs. The ability to stand upright is what separates man from ape. To urinate in any other position is primitive. Flinging feces is also frowned upon.

Urinal Challenge - Height
Often a coming of age for men, how high a man can aim up the urinal is often a sign of how much of a man he is.

Urinal Challenge - Urination Time
Any man standing beside another man at a urinal has automatically engaged himself in combat. The challenge is to urinate for the longest period. No man shall cheer or celebrate winning a pee-challenge; the combat, like other things in the restroom are silent.

Stalls - Stall to Urinal Conversion
For expediency at busy bars and nightclubs, it is conventional to convert a stall to a urinal. This conversion is symbolized by a generous spraying of urine all over the toilet and sometimes the rest of the stall.

Stalls - Loud Crap Noises
Loud crap noises (squirts, butt flapping, etc.) shall be covered up by coughing, sneezing, or banging your fist on the stall. You will gain extra man cards if you scream or grunt loudly while

dropping the browns off at the Super Bowl. Flush when you're done.

Work and Leisure: Transportation

Mans Intuition
A man can and will drive at any chance he gets. Women are not to drive unless its their car, even then only once a month are you aloud to ride passenger to a woman (Like rollover minutes you can save them up for future use). A man can drive any vehicle no matter how sophisticated, without training (this includes harrier jets, 747s and submarines).

Exception: Airbus Planes due to massive scale, and foreign design.

Acceptable problems:
- If your car is in the shop the woman may drive (if its her car)
- Your ability to focus has been severely impeded by alcohol consumption
- You intend on your ability to focus being severly impeded by alcohol consumption

The Basic Rules
If two or more men share a vehicle, the following order of progression is used to find who will drive if both are going to the same place. (calling it doesnt count)
- Health (The most physically fit man will drive)
- Commonality (the most frequent user will drive)
- Girlfriend Bypass (In the event of a user picking up a girlfriend he is automatically given rights to drive the

vehicle even if the other man beats the dating man in #s 1 and 2)

Vehicles
The following vehicles are the preference order as an OPERATOR, in terms of manliness:

Extremely manly, in order:
Space ship, tank, jet fighter, military vehicle (other than tank), motorcycle, horse, airplane, helicopter, sailboat, motorboat, ATV, hot-air balloon, off-roader

Somewhat manly, in order:
Train, semi truck, pickup truck, stick-shift car, bicycle, city bus

Not manly, from best to worst:
automatic transmission car, golf cart, limo, cross-country bus, SUV, motor home

Unmanly, from bad to worse:
Segway, motorized chair, minivan, station wagon, Vespa, Hybrids

Note: Even a hybrid from the manliest category, such as a tank, would be considered unmanly.

Acceptable:
Students may drive automatic transmission, but by age 18 need to learn stick shift.

A man driving a minivan is one of two things: Comfortable with his manhood or driving children. (Occasionally both)

As a PASSENGER, the order of manliness is:
Space ship, military vehicle, motor boat, pickup truck, sailboat, golf cart, limo, train, standard transmission car, SUV, cross-country bus, motor home, minivan, city bus.

Being a passenger in any of the other vehicles listed in the first section is unmanly.

An exception may occur for the minivan if it is the first car you ever owned, was gifted to you by family, and you are under the age of 30. At this point, you will be required to drive something that is either a diesel or has treads

Driving Skills
- No man shall drive slowly in the fast lane. "Slowly" is defined as less than 10 mph over the speed limit.
- No man shall speed up when someone tries to pass. However, if a man is following the previous rule this should not be a problem.
- No man shall slow down after passing someone.
- Driving skills are inherent on the Y chromosome. Failure to demonstrate said skills will result in forfeit of manhood. Your new nickname will be Princess.
- No man should sit forward when operating a motor vehicle. Appropriate postures include the lazy one arm, the Tokyo-Drift double-stiff arm (when racing), and of course,.the road head accommodation position.

- A man must "peel out" whenever given opportunity.
- When given the chance to drive between the man and his girlfriend the man should always drive.
- Hogging the middle lane will result in immediate loss of your man card. If you don't know how to use the road, better let someone else drive, Princess .

Directions

No man shall ask for directions. This standard is derived from women's stereotype of men. Men are to live down to women's expectations. Besides, women don't ask for directions either.

Games - Shotgun

To claim front passenger seat, a man shall be the first to announce 'shotgun'. The driver must be present, along with the majority of passengers. The caller must be outside of the location being left, with the car in view, and cannot go anywhere except to the car once Shotgun is called. If someone has touched the door handle, it is too late. The driver has the right to override shotgun without an explanation.

Games - Slug Bug (Punch Buggy)

Slug Bug is a children's game. No man over the age of 16 shall participate. If you have your licence you aren't a kid anymore. Also, if anyone in the car dares to play the 'Volksvagen Game', it is encouraged to pull over and punish the purpatrator.

Mechanic Skills

The following skills are required in order for a man to be allowed to drive a motor vehicle, or else he must accept the name Princess.

Diesel

A man should be able to determine a diesel engine by sound alone.

Tires

A man MUST be able to change a tire without help.

Oil

A man must know how to check the oil in his vehicle, for both quantity and quality. A man must also have personally changed the oil in at least one vehicle at one time in his life. It is acceptable if he did this with the help of other men as long as (1) he used at least one tool himself and (2) got oil on himself in the process.

Air filter

A man must either have personally changed the air filter on one car in his life, or else have denied permission to change the air filter to at least one Jiffy Lube employee, not withstanding the grease smudge the employee just put on the filter.

WANT ME TO CHANGE YOUR AIR FILTER?

MOVE ASIDE, SON. I GOT THIS.

WALLY WORLD'S AUTO TECH GUY

Car Color

No man should EVER drive a vehicle in any color that can't be found in nature or could be considered girly. Examples:

- Pink
- Turquoise
- Orange
- Sky-Blue

Exceptions:
- Sky-Blue muscle cars with white stripes are acceptable.
- FAB 1 is the only acceptable pink car. Any car that can deploy a machine gun through the radiator grille is manly.
- Orange Corvettes are acceptable so long as it has not been painted orange by the man.
- Orange is also acceptable if the car is a 69 charger with a confederate flag on the roof and also has a name
- Orange is also acceptable if the car is an Italian sports car that can reach over 200mph.

Everything Else: Rules For Women

Entertainment - Television Autopilot
No woman shall converse with a man while he is within line-of-sight of a television. When watching television, a man is in the vulnerable state of autopilot. The man will say anything to get the woman to stop talking, but will not be conscious of what is said. He will not even remember having a conversation.

Entertainment - Television Accountability
No woman shall hold a man accountable for anything he says within line-of-sight of a television. In this altered state of consciousness, a man will say illogical and often misleading things. He will agree to unreasonable demands and have no recollection of doing so. A woman who makes demands of such a vulnerable man is manipulative and should not be trusted.

Entertainment - Video Game Autopilot/Accountability
Flow-like states of autopilot can also be induced by video games. The above two rules apply during states of video-game autopilot.

Entertainment - Chick Flicks

No woman shall require a man to like a chick flick. A man may be willing to watch a chick flick with a woman, provided there is at least some cuddling involved.

Entertainment - Fair Trade

A woman shall suffer through one action movie for every 1/2 of a chick flick she makes a guy suffer though. Men know women do not like action movies, which only further proves their inferiority. Woman know men do not like chick flicks. Nobody cares.

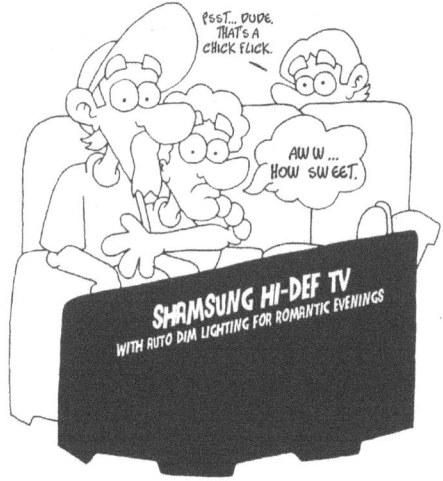

Relationships - Christmas Presents

When asked "What do you want for Christmas?" any woman who replies with, "If you loved me, you'd know what I want," gets a PS3, Alienware Gaming Computer or Xbox One. No questions asked.

Relationships - Thinking

No woman shall ask a man what he is thinking. 90% of the time, he's thinking of nothing. 9% of the time, he's thinking about sex. The last 1% of the time, you don't want to know what he's thinking. If a man answers this question and you like his answer, it's because he's really good at making something up on the fly.

Relationships - Only Possible Answer

There are occasions where telling the truth will lead to absolutely NO good, it can plunge you into the depths of anger, hurt feelings, hysteria, chaos, or any combination af the above. So when a woman asks an impossible question, a man shall give the Only Possible Answer, even if it involves a 'little white lie'. These questions qualify (add to list as you see fit):

- Do these pants make my butt look fat? (Only answer 'Yes' if at a store and she hasn't bought them yet.)
- Do you think she is prettier than me?
- Do you have more fun with your friends than with me?
- Were you looking at HER?!? (Correct answer = "Eww... yeah.")

Style - Chick Mullet

No woman shall bear a mullet, for the chick-mullet (AKA femullet) is more frightening than the dude-mullet.

Style - Femhawk

No woman under any curcumstances shall bear a mohawk, its impractical, you already have our attention, and it takes way too long to get a new hair style.

Work and Leisure - Wrapping Paper

When unwrapping a gift, please tear the wrapping paper. You're not going to reuse it. The only alternative to tearing the wrapping paper is using explosives to obliterate the package. Of course, this technique should only be used on gifts from mother-in-laws and co-workers.

More From A BackPew Review

Thanks for reading this guide. We hope you enjoyed it and will continue to read our other guides in the series. Here is a complete list of our books from the series:

- **What Does It Mean To Be A Christian**
- **Acts: The Early Days Of The Christian Church**
- **Being A Dad According To The Bible**
- **The Prison Letters: Apostle Paul's Letters To The Early Church**
- **Exodus: The Journey To The Promised Land**
- **Genesis: The Beginning, The Fall And The Promise**
- **The Seven Letters: The New Testament Letters To The Early Church**
- **The Gospel From A Four-Sided View**
- **Healthy Eating: A Few Tips From The Bible**
- **Being A Man According To The Bible**
- **A Marriage Built To Last: Learn What The Bible Says About Marriage**
- **How Do I Pray? The Bible Tells Us How**
- **Revelation: The End Is Near?**

Milton Keynes UK
Ingram Content Group UK Ltd.
UKHW040358291024
450367UK00011B/164

9 798330 495016